GREAT LGBTQ+ SPEECHES

This book is dedicated to the affirming
parents of trans-kids everywhere.

GREAT TEA UGLOW
LGBTQ+
SPEECHES

EMPOWERING VOICES THAT INSPIRE + EMPOWER

FOREWORD BY **Peter Tatchell**

WHITE LION PUBLISHING

Quarto

First published in 2020 as *Loud and Proud*
This edition first published in 2022 by White Lion Publishing,
an imprint of The Quarto Group.

One Triptych Place
London, SE1 9SH
United Kingdom
T (0)20 7700 6700
www.Quarto.com

A catalogue record for this book is available from the
British Library.

ISBN 978 0 7112 7500 3
Ebook ISBN 978 0 7112 7502 7

10 9 8 7 6 5 4 3 2

Design by Isabel Eeles

Printed in Lithuania

CONTENTS

FOREWORD
BY
PETER TATCHELL

These speeches are the inspiring, pioneering voices of the persecuted, marginalized, ignored and reviled, who refused to remain cowed and silent, often at great personal risk to their reputation, freedom and safety. Their words rang out to shatter the quiet, to make visible the invisible and to advance a just cause. They demanded nothing more than the most basic of human rights: dignity, respect, acceptance and equality for LGBTQ+ people.

Among the speech givers in *Great LGBTQ+ Speeches* are well-known LGBTQ+ advocates such as Ian McKellen, Sylvia Rivera, Harvey Milk, Audre Lorde, George Takei, Bayard Rustin and Elton John.

But we also hear from little-known champions such as Anna Rüling, the German activist who was the first woman in the world to give a political speech in defence of lesbianism, way back in 1904; Simon Nkoli the black, gay anti-apartheid activist, jailed in South Africa in the 1980s; and Anna Grodzka, Poland's first transgender MP (2011–15).

Alongside them are the speeches of straight allies, who stood with LGBTQ+ people in our long quest for liberation, including Barack Obama, Loretta E. Lynch, Hillary Rodham Clinton and Ban Ki-moon.

Many people too often see the LGBTQ+ emancipation struggle as a post-Stonewall 1969 social movement. We are reminded in this book that it actually stretches back over 150 years to trailblazers that include Karl Heinrich Ulrichs who made a ground-breaking appeal for the decriminalization of homosexuality to the Congress of German Jurists in 1867.

Read this book and be inspired and motivated to support the global struggle for queer freedom. Over one-third of the world's countries still outlaw same-sex relations, and several have the death penalty.

Don't accept the world as it is. Dream of what the world could be – and then help make homophobia, biphobia and transphobia history.

Peter Tatchell

INTRODUCTION
BY
TEA UGLOW

It turns out there is no queer school. Nowhere to learn how to be Lesbian or Gay, or Trans or Queer, let alone Bisexual. No 'right' way to be anything. No one can be too gay, or not gay enough. There are no rules and there is no obligatory queer history. Sometimes that feels like a shame. On the other hand, feminism has spent more than 100 years trying to destroy the 'how to be a woman' school, and we are only just beginning to make inroads with the equally toxic 'how to be a man' school. Yet the absence of a 'how to be queer' canon does leave some rudimentary gaps in one's knowledge. For example, despite starting my queer life very early and arriving very late to my queer self, I never knew that 'homosexual' was originally a German word, nor that the Germans led the way in defining ideas of homosexual human rights in the nineteenth century (see pages 14–17 and 20–23). The first American gay rights movement was established in 1924 by Henry Gerber, a German. I never knew there were ten years of 'lesser' riots and pickets across the United States prior to Stonewall, and that *The Advocate* (the American LGBTQ+ magazine) was founded as a result of one of these. This book is the longer story of how we came to this point in our collective identity. It is not a history book, nor is it a collection of inspirational quotes; there is no hierarchy to it, only a loose chronological timeline allowing for thematic clusters including identity and the fight for societal recognition, the AIDS crisis and its associated stigma, gay marriage and transgender rights and visibility. It features the spoken words of queer people and their allies (and, occasionally, their nemeses). Ideally, it will remind us how powerful it is to look an audience in the eye and tell our truth.

I believe in the political act of storytelling as a way of letting folk know that they are not alone. I believe that being visible is the most helpful thing anyone can do for others. It is an old idea, but it is true.

This message has been repeated throughout history, throughout this book – from Filipino politicians (see pages 148–49) to Iranian activists (see pages 100–01), South African poets (see pages 124–27), camp queens and angry dykes. Repeatedly, the call is to be visible, to be seen and to be heard.

It only occurred to me recently that I was taught to deny and reject my identity. For twenty-five years (between 1988 and 2003) British politicians legislated to make it illegal to teach awareness of LGBTQ+ issues in schools (see pages 60–63). I was completely blind to the history of queer people. As a geeky queer trans-kid I grew up in a barren silo, fumbling around for an identity. It is ironic that the evergreen cliché of LGBTQ+ activists teaching kids to be gay (or trans) is undeniably a fact when seen in reverse: I was taught 'straight' by society. For the vast majority of our speakers in *Great LGBTQ+ Speeches*, this will have been their battle too. A fight not just with their peers and society, but with the intellectual rejection of their existence and deep-rooted feelings of disgust and self-loathing taught to them through their 'education'. Hopefully this book will reach people with the spoken words of our queer heritage.

I have had an unusual process of 'coming out' in my life. I have identified as a closeted gay man, both kinds of straight, a queer woman, asexual, bisexual and then, finally, as pansexual when that became an option. In other words, having been alive for forty years, I have come to the conclusion that labelling bodies with fixed binaries of sexuality and gender is simplistic. Or at the very least, unwise. It leads to conflict, division, prejudice and othering. Yet in most societites it is the norm. But vocabulary and terminology are forever evolving and spoken words have opened doors and changed lives.

There are words in this book that changed lives forever. Words that, once spoken, opened doors that could never be closed. Words that brought tears and understanding, violence and retribution. The bravery of the speakers featured in this book is immense. Often these speeches were made in front of hostile audiences. Words – especially spoken words – matter. They change our world, our lives, our sense of self. And they will continue to do so and fight on.

It may feel like a triumphant story in places, like we have finally arrived but we are nowhere near finished. There are maybe just shy of one billion LGBTQ+ people on the planet; in some countries we may get married, self-identify and live a life of privilege with our siblings. In others, that fight is still heard in the courthouses and tabloids on a daily basis. In yet other countries we still face a death penalty for how we are born. It is worth remembering how privilege has given us that liberty, unlike many brave, less fortunate queer people who continue to fight for the right to say life-changing words such as 'I do' or 'Not Guilty'.

There is a lot of conflict in this book – both external and internal within religious and state structures, but also with each other. Karl Heinrich Ulrichs (see pages 14–17) made the first request for legal recognition of men for whom 'nature has planted in them a sexual nature that is the opposite of that which is in general usual', and Sylvia Rivera (see pages 28–31) raged at her humiliation a century later on Christopher Street, New York City, in front of exactly that group of men. Sally Miller Gearhart (see pages 24–27) ripped into the patriarchy and toxicity of the Christian church orders; Essex Hemphill (see pages 64–67) implored his black gay brothers to come out to their families, just as Harvey Milk (see pages 38–41) begged us all to come out for each other. Audre Lorde (see pages 34–37) laid down, in exquisite poetry, foundations of intersectional feminism that we are still building on today. *Great LGBTQ+ Speeches* should remind us that our collective journey is cyclical and unending. Unity is standing with our allies and fighting for their entitlement just as they fought for you when your people were as disenfranchised.

I have tried to include international voices – those for whom the political cycle may be at a very different stage, both through the nations who have paved the way for equality by selecting queer politicians and heads of state (see pages 120–123) and those who still refuse to recognize the rights of the LGBTQ+ community. State-sponsored persecution and imprisonment of queer people occurs across the world with 73 countries criminalising same-sex activity including Egypt, Pakistan, Cameroon and Iran (see pages 100-01). Trans identities remain unrecognized in most Arab states and are openly reviled in others. Closer to home, in Singapore, a dear friend faces jail time for 'inciting gayness'. Yet is not just seemingly distant locations like Chechnya that require caution – it is outside my house in Sydney or in Brooklyn or Berlin, Tokyo, Paris, Chingford. In a 2012 report, the charity Stonewall found that 41 per cent of British trans people had been attacked or threatened with violence. Gay and queer people are abused, beaten, threatened. It happens daily. It is normal. It is everywhere.

So while this is a Western chronology, a narrative strung around perspectives distilled mainly from English-speaking white LGBTQ+ activists, we have endeavoured to find diverse perspectives. We acknowledge that centring Western colonial voices is far from ideal. Part of that acknowledgement is accepting that the 'history' and the language, critique and the evolution of ideas that we present is itself born out of that privilege. As a movement we must continue to build bridges with other queer histories and cultures all over the world, to fight for rights in countries where that does not exist, where we know no one. We hope that eventually we will know the names and deeds of activists in every corner of the world, and hear their words too.

There are absences for other reasons as well: history is not kind and considerate to the marginalized. Transcribing speeches from lesser-known YouTube clips or multiple press clippings has opened my eyes to the notion of erasure in a vivid, practical way. Many voices are absent, including some that have lifted the hearts of queer people all over the world. They may be under copyright, or simply too fresh and too personal. For example, Hannah Gadsby's (see page 172) performance, Nanette, which is probably one of the most widely seen, powerful and popularly received queer speeches in recent history was not available for this edition. Frankly, I am grateful that I am not expected to find a mere 400 words within it to summarize the show. In an aim to continue the conversation, we have included a selection of some of the inspirational people whose speeches we were unable to include in More Voices to Inspire (see pages 168–71).

Over 150 years our idea of a speech has evolved from printed stump speeches to Netflix specials and grainy YouTube uploads; the location has moved from hostile witness stands to ally-packed award nights. But we still need our heroes to speak up, to find a platform and say the words that shake and shape our community. Thank you to all our speakers, and our absent ones too.

And we left space … for a second edition … because the fight is not over and there are still speeches to be discovered.

We hope you will tell us who we missed and why.

Tea Uglow

As is evident in the speeches in this book, the language surrounding sexual and gender identity is constantly shifting and evolving. We have opted to use the term LGBTQ+ throughout Great LGBTQ+ Speeches *but have refrained from altering the original speech transcripts. You can find further details on the history of the terminology in PinkNews's and Stonewall's glossaries.*

KARL HEINRICH ULRICHS

German Lawyer and Pioneer of the Modern Gay Rights Movement
1825–1895

Modern ideas about homosexuality can be traced back only as far as the nineteenth century. Naturally, there have always been queer people. However, with the birth and subsequent science of 'homosexuality' came the pioneers of the modern gay liberation movement, sparking a revolution that began in Europe and in time spread across the globe.

Probably the most significant openly gay activist of that period was Karl Heinrich Ulrichs. A German jurist of the mid-nineteenth century, his ideas were as naive and complicated as you would expect from the first person to try to form a theory of homosexuality. He devised a whole nomenclature for types of sexuality and identities. A gay man was called an 'Urning' – a term that nearly caught on until an alternative ('homosexual') was coined a few years later.

In 1867, he appeared before the Congress of German Jurists to appeal for the abolition of the sodomy statute. He was met with derision and outrage. Despite being interrupted and unfinished, it is heralded as the first public call for legal recognition for homosexuals. Following this, Ulrichs began to write pamphlets about gay life, in which he emphasized the importance of visibility: 'As Urnings [Queer people], we should and must present ourselves without a mask. Only then will we conquer ground to stand on in human society; otherwise, never.'

Ulrichs stood up and spoke his truth to the world, which led to harassment, imprisonment and finally self-imposed exile in Italy where he died in 1895. The same year, he received an honorary diploma from the University of Naples in recognition of his work. Today, Ulrichs is celebrated with streets named after him and awards given in his name.

Speech to the Congress of German Jurists

Munich

29th August 1867

Gentlemen! Already two years ago a proposal was regularly presented by two members of the Congress, Professor Dr. Tewes of Graz and myself, and I would like in a legal protest to complain that it was suppressed by our deputation, that is to say, it was excluded from the agenda as 'not suitable to be considered by the Congress.' I base my protest on material and formal grounds.

This proposal is directed towards a revision of the current penal law, in particular towards the final repeal of a special, unjust penal regulation that has come down to us from earlier centuries, towards the abolishing of the persecution of an innocent class of persons that is included in this penal regulation. It is at the same time a question of establishing in this point a legal uniformity not present in Germany, since Bavaria and Austria, on the one side, both reject this persecution, while the rest of Germany stands diametrically opposite. Finally, it is also a question, on a secondary level, of damming a continuing flood of suicides, and that of the most shocking kind. I believe that this is indeed a very worthy, serious, and important legal question, with which the Congress of German Jurists may quite suitably be called on to be concerned. It is a question, gentlemen, of a class of persons that indeed in Germany is numbered in the thousands, a class of persons to which many of the greatest and noblest intellects of our and other nations have belonged ...

[cries of 'Stop!']

... which class of persons is exposed to an undeserved legal persecution for no other reason

[More shouting. Including 'Stop! Stop!' from one side of the hall. The chairman calls to put the protest to a vote]

... Under these circumstances I give up the floor and lay my protest on the table.

[From the other side of the hall: 'No, no! Continue, continue!']

... which class of persons is exposed to an undeserved legal persecution for no other reason than that mysteriously disposing creating nature has planted in them a sexual nature that is the opposite of that which is in general usual....

[General commotion and shouting. Chairman: 'I request the speaker to use Latin in continuing!' Ulrichs places his pages on the chairman's table and leaves the platform.]

Under these circumstances I give up the floor and lay my protest on the table.

———————————

Karl Heinrich Ulrichs

ROBERT G. INGERSOLL

American Writer and Orator
1833–1899

Address at the Funeral of Walt Whitman

Harleigh, Camden, New Jersey, USA
30th March 1892

It is worth considering that Walt Whitman – one of the United States's most lauded poets – never personally identified as gay. Indeed, it would have been difficult for him to do so as there was no such word to use in his lifetime. The word 'homosexual' emerged towards the end of the nineteenth century among German sexologists. The word 'gay' had no sexual connotation until the middle of the twentieth century. Lord Alfred Douglas may have penned his famous phrase, 'the love that dare not speak its name', partly because it had no name to dare speak.

With Whitman we have his poetry to account for him, and also decades of romantic correspondence with bus conductor Peter Doyle. However, he could never come out, and he never spoke publicly of it. So we have included the address for Whitman that was given at his funeral by his close friend, the great American orator Robert G. Ingersoll. Ingersoll was a well-known and highly regarded cultural figure in the nineteenth century. A common form of entertainment in the US at the time was gathering and listening to speeches by elderly white men. Ingersoll was particularly talented in this regard. This address is a testimony to a beloved friend; it is an invocation of the spirit and freedom to love. Moving and significant, it is an oblique acknowledgement of Whitman's gentle truth: that he was gay. A truth that could finally exist where before we had nothing, no names, no words at all, only silence.

Again, we, in the mystery of Life, are brought face to face with the mystery of Death. A great man … lies dead before us, and we have met to pay tribute to his greatness and his worth.

I know he needs no words of mine. His fame is secure. He laid the foundations of it deep in the human heart and brain. He was, above all I have known, the poet of humanity, of sympathy. He was so great that he rose above the greatest that he met without arrogance, and so great that he stooped to the lowest without conscious condescension. He never claimed to be lower or greater than any of the sons of men.

He came into our generation a free, untrammeled spirit, with sympathy for all. His arm was beneath the form of the sick. He sympathized with the imprisoned and despised, and even on the brow of crime he was great enough to place the kiss of human sympathy.

One of the greatest lines in our literature is his, and the line is great enough to do honor to the greatest genius that has ever lived. He said, speaking of an outcast: 'Not until the sun excludes you will I exclude you.' His charity was as wide as the sky, and wherever there was human suffering, human misfortune, the sympathy of Whitman bent above it as the firmament bends above the earth.

ANNA RÜLING

German Journalist and Lesbian Activist
1880–1953

Anna Rüling can lay claim to being the archetype of the 'problematic' lesbian. Born into a middle-class German family in the nineteenth century, she defied her family to become a journalist. Some biographers also assume that she began a lesbian relationship, although this is not a recorded fact. In 1904 she was invited to speak at the Scientific Humanitarian Committee (WhK) in Berlin, the first international LGBTQ+ organization.

When you read this speech, consider for a moment that Anna was twenty-four, and that she was the first woman in the world to give a political speech about lesbian identity. Imagine the bravery of this woman standing in front of a hall filled with men, even if they were allies, and saying these words.

Those words (all 5,000 of them) demonstrate all the difficulties that we face when trying to parse nineteenth-century values through a twenty-first-century lens. Eyebrows will rise and eyes will roll. She is particularly harsh on heterosexual women, adopting a fairly toxic line about them being ruled by emotions and fit only to be a wife and mother. Much of it sounds ugly or 'problematic' to our progressive ears.

In some ways, the speech was trolling in nineteenth-century form, provoking the German Women's Movement to acknowledge and even support the lesbian activists in their midst. It is a reminder that often change happens too slowly to remember. Who would have thought that lesbians were excluded by radical feminists? A hopeful note to marginalized groups involved in similar debates today that change does occur, and can even seem absurd, given time.

What Interest Does the Women's Movement Have in Solving the Homosexual Problem?

Berlin, Germany
9th October 1904

Ladies and Gentlemen, the Women's Movement is a historical and cultural necessity. Homosexuality is a historical and cultural necessity, and homosexuality is an obvious and natural bridge between man and woman.

... People in general, when the matter concerns homosexuals ... overlook how many female homosexuals there are. They are, of course, less discussed because they – I was just about to say 'unfortunately' – have had no unjust cause to fight against, such as penal code paragraphs which arise out of having false moral views. No cruel justice menaces women nor does the penitentiary if they follow their natural instincts. But the mental pressure which Urninds [lesbians] suffer is just as great, indeed even greater than the yoke which their male fellow-sufferers must bear.

... If people would just observe, they would soon come to the conclusion that homosexuality and the Women's Movement do not stand opposed to each other, but rather they aid each other reciprocally to gain rights and recognition, and to eliminate the injustice which condemns them on this earth.

... In middle-class circles they believe, oddly enough, that among them homosexuality has no place.... I would like to give as an example, that my father, when by chance he came to speak about homosexuality, explained with conviction, 'nothing of the sort can happen in my family'. The facts prove the opposite. I need to add nothing to that statement.

There are as many good people among homosexuals as among so-called 'normal' people. Most of all, I would like to avoid the appearance of estimating homosexuals too highly. I can assure you, ladies and gentlemen, I will not do that – I am well aware of the problems of homosexuality, but I also recognize its good side.

... I would like to emphasise again that homosexual women have done their part in the greater Women's Movement, that they are mostly responsible for activating the movement....

Without the power and cooperation of the Urninds [lesbians], the Women's Movement would not be so successful today.... The Women's Movement and the movement for homosexual rights have thus far travelled on a dark road which has posted many obstacles in their way.... This is not to say that the work of securing the rights of women and of Uranians [LGBTQ+] has come to an end; we are still in the middle of two opposing sides, and many a bloody battle will have to be fought.

... Perhaps not today or tomorrow, but in the not too distant future the Women's Movement and Uranians [LGBTQ+] will raise their banners in victory!

Homosexuality is a historical and cultural necessity, and homosexuality is an obvious and natural bridge between man and woman.

Anna Rüling

SALLY MILLER GEARHART

American Academic, Sci-Fi Writer and Gay Rights Activist
1931–2021

Sally Miller Gearhart was a pioneer in the field of gender studies and was one of the first openly lesbian women to achieve a tenured academic position, while she was at San Francisco State University, in 1974. Tenure meant that she could not be fired from her position, but two years before this security Gearhart gave an unapologetic and daring speech to an audience of religious ministers at Graduate Theological Union in Berkeley.

Her audience would not have wanted to hear one word of what Gearhart had to say. The fact that she spoke out to such a potentially hostile audience gives you a sense of how vital and passionate the fight was for the right of women to define themselves, and the right to self-define as lesbian. Pioneers like Gearhart were willing to risk their careers to take their argument to the heart of the establishment – in this case, the religious establishment. In 1972, only one small denomination of the Christian Church in the US did not ban homosexuals from serving in the church. Forty-five years later few have progressed very far. This speech was possibly the first open attack on that principle.

The best speeches make you feel them in your bones, make you wonder what it would be like to be there in person. Sally Miller Gearhart's words should be read in full. We do not have space for that here sadly, but it is a reminder of the intensity that comes from literally speaking truth to power. Whenever I read this speech I'm struck by its honesty and defiance against an institution that has traditionally tried to set moral standards and conventions.

The Lesbian And God-The-Father, Or, All The Church Needs Is A Good Lay – On Its Side

Pacific School of Religion at Berkeley, California, USA

February 1972

First, I cannot separate the lesbian from the woman. This is not only because my oppression has been more as a woman than as a lesbian (though that of course is true), but also because, to me, being a lesbian is what really being a woman means. I like to think that the way politically conscious lesbians 'are' in the world today is the way all women were before the tyranny of the patriarchy. To be a lesbian is to be identified not by men or by a society made by men, but by me, by a woman. And the more I am identified by/for me, by/for my own experience, by/for my own values, the more a full woman I feel I become. More and more woman-identified women are emerging everyday....

More and more lesbians. It's not that more and more women are leaping into bed with each other. That may be your fantasy – certainly it is a common male fantasy – as to what lesbianism is all about. And indeed, my understanding is that astounding numbers of women are extending their love relationships with other women into sexual dimensions. But that's not the distinguishing characteristics of a lesbian. Lesbianism is a lifestyle, a mind-set, a body of experience. I would like to call any woman-identified woman a lesbian, and if she's really woman-identified, she'll feel good about being called a lesbian, whether or not she's had any sexual relationship with another woman.

The woman-identified women who are being reborn every day are those who are shaking off the chains forged by thousands of years of ecclesiastical propaganda. Shaking off their definition as male property, as male's helpmate, as the pure and empedestaled virtue-vessels that need chivalrous male protection. They are the unladylike women, the angry women, the ones who make you feel a little uneasy with their freedom of body.... Particularly if you are a man, you both hate and admire their independence, their strength.

The women being reborn today (that's the real meaning of resurrection) are the ones marching for the rights to their own bodies at abortion demonstrations.... They are women whose faces are honest, whose hair flies free, whose minds and bodies are growing supple and steady and sure in self-possession, whose love is growing deep and wide in the realities of newly discovered relationships with other women.

They don't need the Church. The last thing they think about now is the Church. They have within themselves what the Church has claimed as its own and distorted so ironically for its own economic and psychological purposes these thousands of years.

To be a lesbian is to be identified not by men or by a society made by men but by me, by a woman.

Sally Miller Gearhart

SYLVIA RIVERA

American Drag Queen and Transgender Rights Activist
1951–2002

This is the most angry speech and the most upsetting speech in the volume. It is a speech in which a trans woman is heckled by gay men and women, which is where the strange title comes from. You can watch it on YouTube, and you should. It is a powerful moment in the LGBTQ+ collective culture.

The anger comes from Sylvia Rivera, a friend of iconic leader, Marsha P. Johnson, and co-founder of Street Transvestite Action Revolutionaries (STAR). She was probably one of the first to start throwing bottles at police outside the Stonewall Inn in 1969. Rivera was always outspoken, always difficult, magnetic, irresistible and, by nearly all accounts, a force to be reckoned with. In other words: she was exactly what was needed at the time.

If you want to hear the rage and discontent felt by the excluded queer community during the gay political awakening of the 1970s, then her voice expresses it in every syllable. It is cracked and furious with literally everyone. It exposes an unpleasant rift that perhaps, even fifty years later, has not completely resolved – the ugly misogyny of voices raised against gender fluid people, and particularly towards trans women of colour.

This speech, given at Christopher Street four years after the Stonewall riots, broke Rivera and she left activism for two decades, only returning in the 1990s. She died in 2002, still a divisive and difficult character – as many in these pages are – because to be heard when the world does not want to hear you, to raise your voice when every other voice demands your silence, requires qualities of character that are uncommon and hard to manage. Sometimes you just have to scream.

I have been beaten.
I have had my nose broken.
I have been thrown in jail.
I have lost my job.
I have lost my apartment
for gay liberation...

———————————

Sylvia Rivera

Y'all Better Quiet Down

Christopher Street Liberation Day Rally, New York City, New York, USA
24th June 1973

I may be –

[loud booing in the crowd]

Y'all better quiet down. I've been trying to get up here all day for your gay brothers and your gay sisters in jail that write me every motherfucking week and ask for your help and you all don't do a goddamn thing for them.

Have you ever been beaten up and raped and jailed? Now think about it. They've been beaten up and raped after they've had to spend much of their money in jail to get their hormones, and try to get their sex changes. The women have tried to fight for their sex changes or to become women. On the women's liberation and they write 'STAR,' not to the women's groups, they do not write women, they do not write men, they write 'STAR' because we're trying to do something for them.

I have been to jail. I have been raped. And beaten. Many times! By men, heterosexual men that do not belong in the homosexual shelter. But, do you do anything for me? No. You tell me to go and hide my tail between my legs. I will not put up with this shit. I have been beaten. I have had my nose broken. I have been thrown in jail. I have lost my job. I have lost my apartment for gay liberation and you all treat me this way? What the fuck's wrong with you all? Think about that!

... The people are trying to do something for all of us, and not men and women that belong to a white middle-class white club. And that's what you all belong to!

REVOLUTION NOW! Gimme a 'G'! Gimme an 'A'! Gimme a 'Y'! Gimme a 'P'! Gimme an 'O'! Gimme a 'W'! Gimme an 'E'! Gimme an 'R'! [crying] Gay power! Louder! GAY POWER!

FRANKLIN KAMENY

*American Astronomer and
Gay Rights Activist*

1925–2011

American television has given us many mutations of public rhetoric. Franklin Kameny's speech is from a show called *The Advocates*, filmed in 1974, before HIV and AIDS, and forty years before gay marriage was legalized in the US by the Supreme Court. *The Advocates* was an early hybrid between what we might consider a late-night debate show crossed with *Judge Judy*. It certainly would not last in today's high-powered soundbite culture, but it is fascinating to see a platform for almost unimaginably different value systems discussed so calmly in front of a restrained public audience. In this particular show, Kameny delivered the opening address advocating for gay marriage and interrogated the 'experts'.

Kameny was fired from his position as an astronomer in the US Army Map Service by the government for being gay in the late 1950s and became a very visible icon for pre-Stonewall activism. He took a civil rights case against the US government to the Supreme Court and, having lost, devoted the rest of his life to lobbying and agitating for LGBTQ+ rights.

The same episode of *The Advocates* also featured a young Elaine Noble, an 'expert lesbian', who a year later became the first openly gay or lesbian candidate elected to state office in the US.

Should Marriage Between Homosexuals Be Permitted?

The Advocates, Village Theater,
University of California, USA

2nd May 1974

Our society guarantees first class citizenship to all of its citizens, the right of the pursuit of happiness to all of its citizens, and the right to be different and to be unpopular without disadvantage to all of its citizens. Our society does not always respect those rights in practice. Exercise by homosexual couples of the right to marry detracts not one iota from the rights of heterosexual couples to marry. Homosexual marriages interfere with no one individually, and such marriages impair or interfere with no societal interest. In fact, they further some societal interest ... Most important, for many persons a legal marriage is psychologically supportive. The relationship is stabilized by it. For society to accuse us, as it does, of unstable, short-term relationships and then to deny us a powerful means of stabilization is to make their accusation self-fulfilling in a peculiarly vicious way ... Our society belongs to all of its members and segments. It is our society as homosexuals quite as much as yours as heterosexuals ... That equality is what America is all about. It is as simple as that.... The issue at hand is whether the alleged harmful effects of homosexual marriages justify denying civil rights, imposing second-class citizenship and doing psychological damage to some fifteen million American citizens of all ages. The answer is a resounding no because no such harmful effects at all have been shown.

AUDRE LORDE

American Writer, Poet, Academic and Civil Rights Activist
1934–92

Audre Lorde called herself a 'black, lesbian, mother, warrior, poet'. She used those words to reclaim stigmatising terms, to reframe how her audience understood them and, subsequently, herself. What might read today as a list of attributes was, in Lorde's time, a battle cry of defiance that was at the vanguard of intersectional feminism.

Lorde's words endure and haunt us. She reminds us of the battles we each fight in some way or another, and the identities inside each of us that are struggling for affirmation. It almost feels impossible not to find some point of self-identification within her work, even when she is speaking explicitly about black feminism, or, as overleaf, about the significance of standing up and speaking out. The speech is poetry in itself and hard to abridge into this short form. It speaks to fear, and the desire for self-protection, and the consequence of a world wherein all those with something to fear stay silent, mute, while knowing that 'the machine will try to grind you into dust anyway.'

Modern Language Association's 'Lesbian and Literature Panel'

Chicago, Illinois
28th December 1977

I have come to believe over and over again that what is most important to me must be spoken, made verbal and shared, even at the risk of having it bruised or misunderstood. That the speaking profits me, beyond any other effect ...

... To question or to speak as I believed could have meant pain, or death. But we all hurt in so many different ways, all the time, and pain will either change or end. Death, on the other hand, is the final silence. And that might be coming quickly, now, without regard for whether I had ever spoken what needed to be said, or had only betrayed myself into small silences, while I planned someday to speak, or waited for someone else's words ... I began to recognize a source of power within myself that comes from the knowledge that while it is most desirable not to be afraid, learning to put fear into a perspective gave me great strength. I was going to die, if not sooner then later, whether or not I had ever spoken myself. My silences had not protected me. Your silence will not protect you ...

What are the words you do not yet have? What do you need to say? What are the tyrannies you swallow day by day and attempt to make your own, until you will sicken and die of them, still in silence? Perhaps for some of you here today, I am the face of one of your fears. Because I am woman, because I am Black, because

I am lesbian, because I am myself – a Black woman warrior poet doing my work – come to ask you, are you doing yours? And of course I am afraid.

... And that visibility which makes us most vulnerable is that which also is the source of our greatest strength. Because the machine will try to grind you into dust anyway, whether or not we speak. We can sit in our corners mute forever while our sisters and ourselves are wasted, while our children are distorted and destroyed, while our earth is poisoned; we can sit in our safe corners mute as bottles, and we will still be no less afraid...

... Where the words of women are crying to be heard, we must each of us recognize our responsibility to seek those words out, to read them and share them and examine them in their pertinence to our lives ...

... The fact that we are here and that I speak these words is an attempt to break that silence and bridge some of those differences between us, for it is not difference which immobilizes us, but silence. And there are so many silences to be broken.

...it is not difference which immobilizes us, but silence. And there are so many silences to be broken.

———————————

Audre Lorde

HARVEY MILK

American Politician and Gay Rights Activist
1930–78

Harvey Milk was one of the first openly gay elected officials in the United States. He had never appeared to hold strong political views, so his career came as a surprise to some. Following a move from New York City to San Francisco, the charismatic Milk emerged as a champion of the less-conservative side of the Bay area LGBTQ+ community. He became a role model for queer community activism. Milk's home district in San Francisco became a global template for the 'gay village' in the 1970s. A stable and, most importantly, visible gay community built up and transformed the neighbour-hood. In 1970s America, it was hard for people to accept gay men, let alone those in positions of authority and there was open hostility towards gay people.

This speech, known as 'the Hope Speech' was a stump speech for Milk as he campaigned for City Supervisor in 1977. His message was about the power of representation and the importance of visibility. He wanted to demonstrate that the democratic process meant one could elect representatives who were embodiments of any community. This, Milk argued, was the best way to defend LGBTQ+ rights, and win the dignity for which marginalized people have always had to fight. To give each other hope, the community had to speak up, come out, and stand together.

Milk gave this speech from the steps of City Hall during the Gay Freedom Day Parade, which would later become the Gay Pride march. Four months later, on 27th November, he was assassinated in the same building. Despite a short political career, Milk is celebrated for his contribution to the LGBTQ+ movement and, in 2009, was posthumously awarded the Presidential Medal of Freedom.

I personally will never forget that people are more important than buildings.

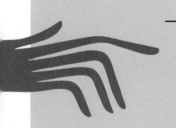

Harvey Milk

The Hope Speech

San Francisco's Gay Freedom Day Parade, California, USA

25th June 1978

You see there is a major difference – and it remains a vital difference – between a friend and a gay person, a friend in office and a gay person in office. Gay people have been slandered nationwide. We've been tarred and we've been brushed with the picture of pornography. In Dade County [Florida], we were accused of child molestation. It's not enough anymore just to have friends represent us. No matter how good that friend may be.

... The anger and the frustrations that some of us feel is because we are misunderstood, and friends can't feel the anger and frustration. They can sense it in us, but they can't feel it. Because a friend has never gone through what is known as coming out. I will never forget what it was like coming out and having nobody to look up toward. I remember the lack of hope – and our friends can't fulfill it.

I can't forget the looks on faces of people who've lost hope. Be they gay, be they seniors, be they blacks looking for an almost-impossible job, be they Latins trying to explain their problems and aspirations in a tongue that's foreign to them. I personally will never forget that people are more important than buildings. I use the word 'I' because I'm proud. I stand here tonight in front of my gay sisters, brothers and friends because I'm proud of you. I think it's time that we have many legislators who are gay and proud of that fact and do not have to remain in the closet. I think that a gay person, up-front, will not walk away from a responsibility and be afraid of being tossed out of office....

And the young gay people ... you have to give them hope. Hope for a better world, hope for a better tomorrow, hope for a better place to come to if the pressures at home are too great. Hope that all will be all right. Without hope, not only gays, but the blacks, the seniors, the handicapped, the "us'es," the "us'es" will give up. And if you help elect to the central committee and other offices, more gay people, that gives a green light to all who feel disenfranchised, a green light to move forward. It means hope to a nation that has given up, because if a gay person makes it, the doors are open to everyone.

So if there is a message I have to give, it is that I've found one overriding thing about my personal election, it's the fact that if a gay person can be elected, it's a green light. And you and you and you, you have to give people hope.

HARRY HAY

Early American Gay Rights Activist, Socialist
and Human Rights Advocate
1912–2002

Harry Hay is best known for his work founding the Mattachine Society, one of the United States's first gay political advocacy groups, and he was a prominent leader in the early gay rights movement. He also led an extraordinary life as a confirmed Marxist throughout the 'red threat' era of McCarthyism, and was equally active in the slow emancipation of gay men from police victimization. He was highly critical of the 'mainstreaming' of gay culture, and generally associated with a variety of groups and political views that made him both a radical and even an outcast.

Ultimately, Hay came to be considered an elder of the queer community and a highly regarded figure who was invited frequently to speak and appear at gay events. This speech, in which Hay discusses the state of the gay rights movement in the mid-1980s, was delivered at the Boston Gay Pride Day Rally. Hay's core belief was that queer culture was distinct from 'normality' and should not seek to assimilate itself within straight culture. He opposed the increased marginalization by gay rights groups of fringe groups (such as polygamy or leather or gender-non-conforming people). Social acceptance of gay people was not worth the sacrifice of our own to him. Some of that criticism can be read through the lyrical imagery of this poetic speech.

...explosions shattered the door-locks of the Hetero Society's closets and attics to reveal that we gay and lesbian folk were indeed everywhere.

_____

Harry Hay

Unity and More in '84

Boston, Massachusetts, USA

30th June 1984

If any of you come to Los Angeles for the Olympics next month, some gay person, taking you on a tour of gay Los Angeles, might drive you to the brow of a hill overlooking the east side of a quiet, silvery lake. On a November afternoon, 34 years ago [1951], five politically radical Gay Brothers sat down together on that hill....

... The moment the New Minority was cut out, pasted together, and stood up on its teetery feet, it took off like a feather in the wind on a life of its own, inviting us to seek cracks and crevices in the heretofore impregnable walls of prejudice imprisoning us, through which our pent-up energies ... now suddenly illuminated by political thought and direction ... might at last begin to flow.

... When the committed five of us swelled to a sphere of influence of possible 5,000 in the State of California by the Spring of 1953, even in the teeth of the McCarthy witch-hunt, we were in trouble. The majority – now middle class in outlook – swamped our radical perceptions and opted for the notion that we were the same as everybody else except in bed.... The bright dreams of rediscovering ourselves died; as the dreams died, our sphere of influence plummeted from 5,000 to 500. And though we laid little powder trains here and there ... the middle-class cop-out remained largely the Movement's policy and outlook until Stonewall. The Stonewall eruption ignited the powder trains we radicals had been laying in many parts of the country. The combined explosions shattered the door-locks of the Hetero Society's closets and attics to reveal that we gay and lesbian folk were indeed everywhere. Gay lifestyles and gay-positive ways of being ourselves suddenly became visible all over the place.

But the ways and means of communicating to the Hetero Society around us as to how we wished to be seen in terms of this new visibility, to be heard, were still not forthcoming....

BAYARD RUSTIN

American Civil Rights Leader and Activist
1912–87

Bayard Rustin was a campaigner and strategist who was arguably straight-washed out of the history of American civil rights movement of the 1960s. He was the organizer of the 1963 March on Washington, one of the largest non-violent protests of that time, and was an advisor to Martin Luther King, Sr. Rustin advocated strongly for King to adopt a position of unilateral non-violent protest – something we now consider part of King's legacy. Despite his achievements, Rustin's name is not as well known as many of his contemporaries.

Encyclopedic records may document his life, but relatively few reference his sexuality. While we all aspire to reach a point where such labels are meaningless to society, in Rustin's America this was certainly not the case. Homophobia was endemic and Rustin lost jobs, leadership positions, was beaten and arrested, and suffered countless indignities doubled for his sexuality and his race.

Perhaps Rustin was not the soaring orator that made King globally famous, but his words, and his strength should not be overshadowed. He stands alone as one of the first openly gay black men and one of the few gay black men who seemed able to speak their own truth to their own community. Rustin was a truly astonishing man who refused to be cowed or closeted. It is never too late to offer a spotlight to quieter heroes, the ones who did not blaze so brightly in the public eye.

This speech was given to a group of gay student activists at the University of Pennsylvania and was later adapted for print.

We have to fight for legislation wherever we are, to state our case clearly...

Bayard Rustin

From Montgomery to Stonewall

University of Pennsylvania, Philadelphia, Pennsylvania, USA

Unknown 1986

In 1955 when Rosa Parks sat down and began the Montgomery Bus Protest, if anyone had said that it would be the beginning of a most extraordinary revolution, most people, including myself, would have doubted it.

Consider now gay rights. In 1969, in New York of all places, in Greenwich Village, a group of gay people were in a bar. The events began when several cops moved into the bar to close it down, a very common practice in that period, forcing many gay bars to go under-ground. The cops were rough and violent, and, for the first time in the history of the United States, gays, as a collective group, fought back and not just that night but the following night, and the next, and the night after that.

Gay people must continue this protest. This will not be easy, in part because homosexuality remains an identity that is subject to a 'we/they' distinction. People who would not say, 'I am like this, but black people are like that,' or 'we are like this, but women are like that,' or 'we are

like this, but Jews are like that,' find it extremely simple to say, 'homosexuals are like that, but we are like this.' That's what makes our struggle the central struggle of our time, the central struggle for democracy and the central struggle for human rights. If gay people do not understand that, they do not understand the opportunity before them, nor do they understand the terrifying burdens they carry on their shoulders.

Well, what do we have to do that is concrete? We have to fight for legislation wherever we are, to state our case clearly, as blacks had to do in the South when it was profoundly uncomfortable. Some people say to me, 'Well, Mr. Rustin, how long is it going to take?' Let me point out to you that it doesn't take a law to get rid of a practice. The NAACP [National Association for the Advancement of Colored People] worked for sixty years to get an anti-lynch law in this country. We never got an anti-lynch law, and now we don't need one. It was the propaganda for the law we never got that liberated us.

SUE HYDE

American Director of the National LGBTQ Task Force (1986-2017) and Executive Director of the Wild Geese Foundation (2018-present)
b. 1952

We Gather in Dubuque

Dubuque Gay and Lesbian Pride Parade, Iowa, USA
30th April 1988

In 1987, amid the hysteria of AIDS-era media coverage, Dubuque's gay community held its first annual Gay and Lesbian Pride Parade. Since Dubuque is a small city in Iowa, in the centre of the United States, there were only thirty people in the parade. These thirty proud marchers were pelted with rocks, refuse and eggs, and were harassed by locals while the police looked on and did nothing. The following year the organizers called for support and more than 600 LGBTQ+ people attended from all over the country in a display of solidarity, shocking the residents of the city.

During the rally, Sue Hyde, the director of the National Gay and Lesbian Task Force (NGLTF), used her speech to talk directly to the people of Dubuque and, through them, to the people of America. It was a short and powerful speech that captured the determination and fierce energy of an LGBTQ+ community that was under extreme duress. Often a speaker asks their audience to show compassion or empathy. In this speech Hyde challenged the Iowan city to be 'the best city it can be'.

We gather in Dubuque today so that none of us will ever feel afraid to walk this city's streets ... [last year's marchers] vowed to return this year because they would not simply bow down to the way Dubuque is. They did not agonize: they organized. And a wonderful thing happened. Ginny Lyons and Stacy Neldaughter, with their spark of courage, lit a fire of resistance and fueled a movement of gay men and lesbians to ... stand with them today.

Dubuque has a special responsibility to make this city safe for [everyone], and to make last year's disgrace this year's triumph. No more harassment. No more eggs or rocks or ugly words. No more governmental neglect and malevolence. No more fear. No more hate. No more silence. We choke on your hatred. We smother under your fear ... And we cannot wait any longer to live.

With one voice, as one people ... we say to you that our time for freedom has arrived. We promise to return to Dubuque each year until we no longer need to. We invoke the spirits of Mahatma Gandhi, Fannie Lou Hamer, Martin Luther King and Barbara Deming, all of whom devoted their lives to freedom and justice. We call on them to guide us, walk with us, and join our one voice as we say: We won't give up. We won't shut up. We won't go away. And we will change this world.

VITO RUSSO

American Author, Historian and Founder of GLAAD
1946–90

Vito Russo could be known as a vocal, colourful, archetypal
'gay activist', a prolific member of ACT UP (AIDS Coalition to
Unleash Power), and as a co-founder of GLAAD (Gay and Lesbian
Alliance Against Defamation – an organization that watches media
representation of LGBTQ+ folk). He is probably better known as
the author of *The Celluloid Closet* (1995), a seminal work on the
history of queer representation in film that catalogued gay and
lesbian appearances on screen up to the late 1980s. *The Celluloid
Closet* was very influential in showing how the treatment and
portrayal of LGBTQ+ people had influenced societal attitudes
towards homosexuality.

Russo's 1988 speech was less to do with cinema and more to do
with life, and death. It needs to be read alongside Mary Fisher's
1992 speech, 'A Whisper of AIDS' (see pages 56–59), which is the
white, heterosexual echo of life in the trenches. The Russo speech
is straight from the frontline, an exhortation to the activists in the
trenches. It spits with indignation, pain and amazement that LGBTQ
people could be so dehumanized: 'It's not happening to us in the
United States, it's happening to them – to the disposable populations
of fags and junkies who deserve what they get.'

He was not alone in this sentiment.

Why We Fight

ACT UP Demonstration, New York State, USA

9th May 1988

You know, for the last three years, since I was diagnosed [with HIV], my family thinks two things about my situation. One, they think I'm going to die, and two, they think that my government is doing absolutely everything in their power to stop that. And they're wrong, on both counts.

... So, if I'm dying from anything, I'm dying from homophobia. If I'm dying from anything, I'm dying from racism. If I'm dying from anything, it's from indifference and red tape, because these are the things that are preventing an end to this crisis. If I'm dying from anything, I'm dying from Jesse Helms [an American politician]. If I'm dying from anything, I'm dying from the president of the United States. And, especially, if I'm dying from anything, I'm dying from the sensationalism of newspapers and magazines and television shows, which are interested in me, as a human interest story – only as long as I'm willing to be a helpless victim, but not if I'm fighting for my life.... I'm dying from anything – I'm dying from the fact that not enough rich, white, heterosexual men have gotten AIDS for anybody to give a shit. You know, living with AIDS in this country is like living in the twilight zone. Living with AIDS is like living through a war which is happening only for those people who happen to be in the trenches. Every time a shell explodes, you look around and you discover that you've lost more of your friends, but nobody else notices. It isn't happening to them. They're walking the streets as though we weren't living through some sort of nightmare. And only you can hear the screams of the people who are dying and their cries for help. No one else seems to be noticing.

...if I'm dying from anything, I'm dying from homophobia.

Vito Russo

MARY FISHER

American HIV Activist, Artist and Author
b. 1948

Mary Fisher seems an unlikely speaker and activist for HIV awareness. She was described by the *New York Times* as a 'rich, white, heterosexual and high-caste Republican'. Diagnosed HIV-positive from her second husband, Mary was invited to speak on the issue at the 1992 Republican National Convention in Houston.

We have several speeches by allies in this collection. Most are actively supportive, but some are accidental allies. In this speech, Fisher is addressing non-allies on an issue that is central to the LGBTQ+ community. In it she quotes Martin Niemöller's poem 'First they came'. The allusion is to the HIV virus' ambivalence towards sexuality, but it was aimed directly at the heart of a US political establishment that thought itself immune, and had exacerbated the crisis. *The New York Times* said the speech left the Convention hall 'in silence, and in some cases, tears'.

Fisher went on to be a vocal activist and campaigner, and continues to live a long life. However, on this day she almost certainly believed she had a death sentence. Most of the audience would have assumed, through ignorance, that she would die soon. So we can read this as a parting message. Very few speeches in this book end with 'God bless the children, and God bless us all'. This speech is a reminder that some audiences can only hear messages from certain people. It is likely that the Republican Party of 1992 could only hear this message from Mary Fisher. We are lucky that she stood to speak on behalf of HIV-positive people the world over, and that she did so with such a poignant and powerful form.

A Whisper Of AIDS

Republican Convention, Houston, Texas, USA

19th August 1992

I have come tonight to bring our silence to an end. I bear a message of challenge, not self-congratulation. I want your attention, not your applause.

I would never have asked to be HIV positive, but I believe that in all things there is a purpose; and I stand before you and before the nation gladly.... [the] AIDS virus is not a political creature. It does not care whether you are Democrat or Republican; it does not ask whether you are black or white, male or female, gay or straight, young or old.

Tonight, I represent an AIDS community whose members have been reluctantly drafted from every segment of American society. Though I am white and a mother, I am one with a black infant struggling with tubes in a Philadelphia hospital. Though I am female and contracted this disease in marriage and enjoy the warm support of my family, I am one with the lonely gay man sheltering a flickering candle from the cold wind of his family's rejection.

... HIV asks only one thing of those it attacks: Are you human? And this is the right question. Are you human? Because people with HIV have not entered some alien state of being. They are human. They have not earned cruelty, and they do not deserve meanness. They don't benefit from being isolated or treated as outcasts....

Someday our children will be grown.... I may not be here to hear their judgments, but I know already what I hope they are. I want my children to know that their mother was not a victim. She was a messenger. I do not want them to think, as I once did, that courage is the absence of fear. I want them to know that courage is the strength to act wisely when most we are afraid. I want them to have the courage to step forward when called by their nation or their party and give leadership, no matter what the personal cost.

HIV only asks one thing of those it attacks: Are you human?

Mary Fisher

SIR IAN MCKELLEN

Noted British Film and Stage Actor
b. 1939

Sir Ian McKellen to many, is Gandalf, from the film version of Tolkein's *Lord of the Rings*. In his long international career on stage and screen he is generally considered one of the finest actors of his time, and is a much-loved figure in his native Great Britain. He came out to the public as gay in 1988 in response to government legislation (Section 28) that sought to oppress LGBTQ+ rights.

Section 28 refers to an infamous clause in a British government bill from 1988 about local government funding. The BBC reported that it 'set alarm bells ringing among people in the theatre, the visual arts, the cinema, music, museums and libraries'.

The clause was nominally intended to restrict a few London Education authorities from promoting gay-friendly literature. However it was clear that it had the potential to create (which it ultimately did) a culture of fear and hysteria that would lead to the silencing of any conversation around the topics of homosexuality within schools and culture for twenty years. It was described, again by the BBC, as 'a backdoor reintroduction of censorship'.

Twenty-one years after the passing of the liberalizing Sexual Offences Act of 1967, this sudden intolerance towards gay people took many by surprise, but the movement had powerful supporters in the established media. *A Sunday Telegraph* editorial suggested that being gay had become 'a bold and brazen, proselytising cult'. It cannot pass without mention that the rhetoric utilized is almost identical to the hysteria being created in 2018 and 2019 around the role and position of trans people, especially trans women in British society.

McKellen came out, both in the traditional sense and as an activist, to speak repeatedly and vehemently about the threat of the bill, which would, by the time of this speech, have become an act of law. In this speech, his charm and easy humour of a natural raconteur cannot hide bitterness and the disbelief that the bill had passed into law. He seems not to have believed that something so inhumane could happen. At that time no one could know quite how damaging this clause would be to the generation of queer children growing up in the United Kingdom.

On Section 28

July 1988

There is a sidenote published alongside Section 28 in Hansard – a little précis to clarify its intention for the casual reader, by which I mean the 600-odd members of Parliament and the even odder noble lords and ladies who create the laws in this democracy of ours: 'prohibition on promoting homosexuality by teaching or by publishing material'.

... This misleading sidenote suggests that Section 28 is only concerned with teaching, with schools and the goings-on going on in them. It refers to the apparent origins of the clause and the claimed motives of those who introduced it....

It is no surprise to discover that this government is philistine.... But one mightn't have expected a government so concerned with education to be itself so careless of words, so illiterate.

... The truth is that homosexuality cannot be taught any more than it can be caught. If heterosexuality could be promoted, there would be no homosexuals, no bisexuals. Everywhere in the media, in the Church, in the teaching of literature, language, art and politics, heterosexuality is daily, hourly promoted. I still haven't been persuaded....

Just consider, when Section 28 becomes law next month, were I to return to this building, licensed by your local authority, could I not be accused of glamorising homosexuality by saying as I do today that 'I'm proud to be gay'? Henceforward any meeting of lesbians and gays in a youth club, every helpline, every night at Heaven [a famous gay nightclub in London] – all are now unsafe ...

Parents had complained that if their kids read about gays they'd be turned into them – the sort of logic which might claim that teaching French encourages emigration. The nation was frightened. Frightened of poofs. Gay activists were to blame for the backlash against them. 'If you don't complain, there'll be nothing for you to complain about.' I'm not sure that anyone mentioned AIDS. A three-line whip managed a majority of 80-odd.

... Where are we now? Are we heading back to 1967? ...

One old campaigner who advised Leo Abse and Lord Arran in 1967 tells me all his work is in vain, but he shouldn't despair. He's forgotten that the law was changed to bring gays out from the tyranny of blackmail so that they might be cured of their disease. That, unbelievably, was the main argument. Five months ago 20,000 lesbians and gays, freely and peaceably marched through Manchester in the biggest crowd assembled there for the last ten years. This Saturday in London twice as many will do the same. There is no going back.

The truth is that homosexuality cannot be taught any more than it can be caught.

Sir Ian McKellen

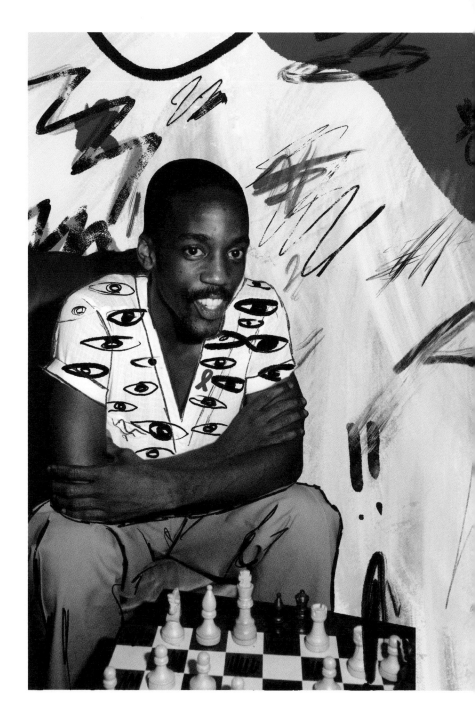

ESSEX HEMPHILL

Poet, American Black and Gay Rights Activist
1957–95

Essex Hemphill was a African-American poet. His speech begins by moving curiously between a vision of black families who cast out and disowned their offspring during the AIDs crisis and a critique of Robert Mapplethorpe, a white gay photographer who did, certainly, objectify his subjects and perhaps his black male subjects, more so than his female or white gay male subjects. Neither are the point of the speech, however. The sharp end of the speech is reserved for his experience of white gay culture that behaves exactly that same way towards black gay men, both objectifying and excluding them. That black gay men are not truly welcome, not truly family. It is a very powerful and troubling speech that reaches hard, difficult conclusions about which community Hemphill needs to come home to.

   This speech can be seen on YouTube, so you can hear Hemphill and understand the poetry, the cadence, the rhythm of his voice as he speaks his words. Then you need to watch it again to understand how furious he was (because you would not know). Then you need to watch it again to understand why he was so furious, why so sad, why what he was saying was ripping him apart, because he felt he had to choose between two families, both of which were failing him in different ways. It is possibly the quietest, most brutal speech in the book and deserves to be read or watched in full.

Untitled. On Mapplethorpe and the Black Penis

OUTWRITE – a conference of gay and lesbian writers, San Francisco, USA
March 1990

Throughout the 1980s many of us grieved the loss of friends, lovers, and relatives who were once strong, healthy, and able-bodied. But then in an instant they became thin-framed, hacking and wheezing, their bodies hacked with horrible pain. Sometimes brave souls would return to the family roots to disclose their sexuality and ask permission to die in familiar surroundings.... Some parents said they always had known while others had never suspected that their son was a black gay man: a sissy, a queer, a faggot.

... The white gay community of the 1980s was not seriously concerned with the plight of black men, except as sexual objects. The black male was given very little representation, except most often as a big black dick. This aspect of white gay consciousness is best revealed by the photographs of the late Robert Mapplethorpe ... Mapplethorpe's eye pays special attention to the penis at the expense of showing us the subject's face, and thus a whole person ... What is insulting and endangering to black men on one level is Mapplethorpe's conscious determination that the faces, the heads, and, by extension, the minds and experiences of some of his black subjects were not as important as close-up shots of their penises.

... These types of pleasure [bathhouses, bars, etc.] were more tolerable with the presence of black men because they enhanced the sexual and the arts. But the same tolerance did not always apply once the sun began to rise. Open fraternizing at a level suggesting companionship or love between the races was not tolerated in the light of day.

... Terms such as Danger Queen ... and Snow Queen ... were created by a gay community that could obviously not be trusted to believe its own rhetoric concerning brotherhood, fellowship, and dignity ... Only a community's silent complicity and racial apathy is capable of reinforcing these issues. Some of ... the best gay minds of my generation would have us believe that AIDS has bought the gay community closer together.... That is only a partial truth which further underscores the fact that the gay community still operates from a one-eyed, one-color perception of community.

... We cannot witness this in silence and apathy and claim our hands are bloodless. We are a wandering tribe that needs to go home before home is gone.

I ask you brothers, does your momma really know about you? Does she really know who I am? Does she know I want to love her son and care for him, nurture and celebrate him? Do you think she'll understand? I hope so, because I am coming home. There is no place else to go that would be worth so much effort and love.

...The white gay community of the 1980s was not seriously concerned with the plight of black men, except as sexual objects.

———————————

Essex Hemphill

SIMON NKOLI

South African Anti-Apartheid and Gay Rights
Activist and Founder of the GLOW Movement
1957–98

First South African Gay and Lesbian Pride March

Johannesburg, South Africa
13 October 1990

The first Pride march in South Africa took place in Johannesburg on 13th October 1990. It was not a huge event, although according to local press it had 'all the accompanying razzmatazz' as over 800 people passed through the streets. It rained on the parade that still tried to raise the spectre of gay oppression that existed alongside apartheid. Alongside, but not hand-in-hand. The parade was notable partly because being gay was so heavily stigmatized that 'presence' was prioritized over 'pride' and some marchers wore paper bags on their heads to conceal their identity.

For Simon Nkoli, the charismatic founder of the GLOW (Gay and Lesbian Organization of the Witwatersrand) movement, it was a pivotal moment. Recently released after four years in prison as part of the Delmas Treason Trial, Nkoli emerged as an openly gay black political leader in South Africa. In prison he had come out to other anti-apartheid leaders as gay, and was diagnosed as HIV positive, another label he chose to wear openly until his premature death in 1998.

His speech is powerful because it is so obvious. Nkoli cuts through the deep, painful complexity of the time to explain that intersectional oppression cannot simply be compartmentalized and he shares a vision for their country where homophobia would be as unthinkable as racism or sexism. It seems straightforward, yet also implicates mechanisms of control that would ultimately be employed again in the oppression of less visible minorities.

This is what I say to my comrades in the struggle who ask me why I waste time fighting for moffies. And this is what I say to gay men and lesbians who ask me why I spend so much time talking about apartheid, when I should be fighting for gay rights.

I am black, and I am gay. I cannot separate the two parts of me into secondary and primary struggle. They will all be one struggle. In South Africa I am oppressed as a black person. And I am oppressed because I am gay. So when I fight for my freedom, I must fight both oppression[s]. All intolerance, all injustice.

… A lot of people are asking why are you making such a fuss now? … Now, we are on the verge of a new South Africa. Now we are in the process of planning a non-racist, non-sexist future, and the protection of gay and lesbian rights must be part of that planning.

We are … evaluating the way the system built walls around us, putting us in our little boxes and telling us to stay there and be quiet.

Well … as a gay man, I am telling the system that I will no longer stay in a little box in the closet. I will come out and assume my rightful place in society. We will all come out and assume our rightful places in society … The laws that make loving a criminal offence must go…. Now.

URVASHI VAID

*American Attorney and Social Justice and
LGBTQ+ Rights Campaigner*
b. 1958

Speech at the March on Washington

Washington, D.C., USA

25th April 1993

Urvashi Vaid is a significant figure in recent LGBTQ+ advocacy in the US and has spent a life involved in leadership roles across the community. Vaid is the sort of hero that the LGBTQ+ community could celebrate more but is sometimes overlooked – perhaps because her work often takes place in the background. Speaking from a marginalized position as both an Asian-American and a lesbian, her messages are direct and challenging.

In the last decade Vaid has talked more regularly about the need for the LGBTQ+ community to address its own unconscious biases. She has pointed out that lip service is paid to the disenfranchised in our community (often along the lines of race and privilege) while doing little – she critiques her own community for taking no concrete action to give those groups equity. 'That means low-income LGBT people, transgender people and our community's women, whose rights are getting the crap kicked out of them, parts of our community across the board – kids, old gay people'. For thirty years she has been a challenging and important voice. This speech, however, is from twenty-six years ago, in a different political landscape. At the National Gay and Lesbian Task Force, in 1993, Vaid stood to speak and gave us this powerful and prescient warning of the rise of right-wing America. A conversation that is still not over.

Hello lesbian and gay Americans. I am proud to stand before you as a lesbian today. With hearts full of love and the abiding faith in justice, we have come to Washington ... to defend our honor and win our equality. But most of all we have come in peace and with courage to say, 'America, this day marks the end from exile of the gay and lesbian people ... For on this day, with love in our hearts, we have come out ... across America to build a bridge of understanding, a bridge of progress, a bridge as solid as steel, a bridge to a land where no one suffers prejudice because of their sexual orientation, their race, their gender, their religion, or their human difference.'

... The extreme right, which has targeted every one of you and me for extinction ... Language itself fails in this task, my friends, for to call our opponents 'The Right', states a profound untruth. They are wrong – they are wrong morally, they are wrong spiritually, and they are wrong politically ... When all of us who believe in freedom and diversity see this gathering, we see beauty and power. When our enemies see this gathering, they see the millennium. Perhaps The Right is right about something. We call for the end of the world as we know it. We call for the end of racism and sexism and bigotry as we know it. For the end of violence and discrimination and homophobia as we know it ... We stand for freedom as we have yet to know it, and we will not be denied.

ERIC ROFES

American Gay Rights Activist, Teacher and Writer
1954-2006

Eric Rofes was first fired from his teaching job for being gay in the late 1970s, and while he continued to be an educator, he also became a significant influence on the narrative that we use to describe the reality of our lives. Rofes' voice had always had that critical, self-referential observation since before the AIDS movement decimated so many, and his was one of the first to start to push back at the victim culture that manifested itself during the 'crisis' and one of the first to insist that not only was the crisis over, but that the gay community had to change the way it is perceived and the way in which it represents itself.

Rofes' 1997 NGLTF (National Gay and Lesbian Task Force) speech was important for highlighting how the community sought to segue back into the world that would continue to exist after AIDS; how it reframed such a traumatic event for a generation that needs to know but does not need to relive the trauma of that time. It is about what happens after the dead have been buried, the corpses cleared, the tears dried and the devastation forgotten by the mainstream. It was a speech that talked to the much less emotive and more practical importance of building a reality for the survivors and for future generations, and their relationship to sex, kink and queer modes of thought. It was a peculiar backlash to a backlash that highlighted how important sexual expression is as part of the LGBTQ+ identity, and that the continued fight for sexual emancipation is more than AIDS, and a corollary to more conservative battles, such as the right to marriage.

The Emerging Sex Panic Targeting Gay Men

National Gay and Lesbian Task Force's (NGLTF) Creating Change
Conference in San Diego, California, USA
16th November 1997

We are seeing the machinery and the power to transform ideology into action emerging in media frenzies over gay men's sex, the conceptualization of current health problems as public health emergencies, the use of exceptional measures to restrict sex spaces by public officials, and extreme actions by police officers and other representatives of state power to curtail the sexual activity and drug use of gay men....

This is precisely what makes the current debates problematic and why many have such powerful feelings of rage and betrayal: 20 years ago we heard Anita Bryant and Paul Cameron insisting gay male sex is diseased and suicidal and these days we hear gay men saying the exact same thing. 20 years ago we fought heterosexuals in the mainstream media who invaded our sex spaces and wrote lurid, uninformed accounts of our sex cultures. These days it's gay men working in the mainstream media who invade the spaces and write the same lurid stories....

Those of us standing up for sexual freedom are neither lost in a romanticized version of the golden age of the 1970s nor dick-hungry men who are selfishly seeking more power and more privilege. We have been condescendingly characterized as immature children who haven't grown up and need to get with the times, put our pricks back in our pants, and apply our energies to the real challenges facing our communities....

Please consider three ... points.

1. Regardless of your confusion or misgivings, stand up firmly against any efforts which mobilize arms of the state to restrict the right of sexual and reproductive self-determination. You don't like sex clubs, don't go to sex clubs. But do not ask your local authorities to shut them down. You don't like sex areas in parks, don't go to sex areas in parks, but don't invite police to bust the men who enjoy such activities.

2. Refuse to cast off any section of our community in order to gain privileges and social acceptance. Demand a continuing commitment to a pluralistic vision of community. Resist scapegoating subcultures you don't know and you don't understand.

3. Try to understand the historic role sex cultures have played in the formation of queer identities and communities and resist seeing them simply as an unfortunate by-product of antigay oppression. Are our sex cultures evidence of our stigmatization, abuse, and reprobation? ...

Perhaps the real trouble with gay men's sex cultures, in a time when many in our communities are replicating heterosexual patterns of social organization, is that they alone give testimony to the fact that gay men as a class have not completely assimilated.

Resist scapegoating subcultures you don't know and you don't understand.

Eric Rofes

ELIZABETH TOLEDO

American Civil Rights Activist

Life, Liberty, and the Pursuit of Happiness: The GLBT Movement at a Crossroads

Washington, D.C., USA

25th April 2000

It is hard to know whether to consider Elizabeth Toledo a queer speaker or an ally. Her speech given in Washington, D.C. in 2000 was delivered during a time when she openly and actively identified as lesbian but in the twenty years that followed she spoke solely on women's issues. Toledo had come out a year earlier and was five days into her tenure as director of the National Gay and Lesbian Task Force (NGLTF). She had never previously led or worked within an LGBTQ+ organization, so this speech was a remarkable debut.

This lack of clarity helps to remind us that while sometimes the power of a speech is in the performance, sometimes the speech is the speech. The labels we attach to the individual, the context and framing of an event can give way to the words. Toledo's speech was strong, important and timely – and, just as we do not know how to categorize the speaker, this was a moment in queer history where the lines between social and legal acceptance had become blurry, where assimilation and acceptance was available to some but not to others. It created opportunities as well as divisions that would frame queer politics to the present day.

There is a checkerboard quality to the legal and cultural victories for the LGBT movement ... the difference between legitimacy and illegitimacy in the eyes of society may rest on something as arbitrary as a state boundary. Many residents of this country assume that the great strides of the civil rights movement have afforded broad protection against discrimination for all. In fact the legal reality is that those of us in same sex relationships have not been fully protected from discrimination in housing, jobs, family law, education – virtually every aspect of our lives is subject to discrimination and, sadly, hate violence or harassment remains a reality in every state in the nation.... The National Gay and Lesbian Task Force frequently receives phone calls from same-sex couples asking for a list of states in which they can legally marry. These individuals ... assume, like many heterosexual Americans, that the barriers of discrimination have been eradicated. The reality, of course, is quite different. Not a single state allows same-sex marriage. Thirty-nine states allow [LGBT] employees to be fired ... Twenty-eight states lack hate crime laws that include sexual orientation....

The GLBT voting bloc has proven to be one of the most powerful constituencies in the country ... we could have the opportunity to shape ground-breaking legal protection.

TAMMY BALDWIN

American Politician
b. 1962

Tammy Baldwin holds many of the 'first' landmarks for gay women in American politics. In 1992 she became the first woman elected to represent Wisconsin and in 1998 the first openly gay woman in Congress. More recently, in 2012, she became the first openly LGBTQ+ person elected to the United States Senate. Although we can assume that other queer senators have existed in the 230-year history of the upper chamber, overall queer representation is notable by its absence in either house. The Republican's last gay congressman (Jim Kolbe) departed in 2006.

Baldwin's record on LGBTQ+ issues is not as weighty as her work on expanding health care or other issues, and perhaps it is notable that one's sexual identity no longer needs to tie one to a cause. In this speech, Baldwin spoke eloquently of her journey through the eyes of a proud lesbian, and of the hope she had seen for a fairer future grow stronger over her career. She concluded with a powerful call to action, that the change we wish to see is in our own hands.

Never Doubt

The National Mall, Washington, D.C., USA

30th April 2000

If I close my eyes, I can remember being here in 1987. I came to this city, this historic place, these steps. Why did I march? I was twenty-five years old.... I was out.... And at that moment of decision I was at once terrified and free. So I marched ... to replace my fear with courage, my isolation with belonging, my anger with hope.

... Now, with open eyes, I am experiencing this march. I come to this city, this historic place, these steps. I am 38 years old and I am a Member of Congress. Why do I march? I march to challenge ... the keepers of the status quo. And I march for a promising and inspiring and incredible new generation of activists so that they might replace their fear with courage, their isolation with belonging, their anger with hope. And I can say with conviction: Never doubt that there is reason to be hopeful.

... Never doubt that the states will grant us equal rights, including all the rights afforded to couples through marriage.

... Never doubt that America will one day realize that her gay, bisexual, and transgendered sons and daughters want nothing more – and nothing less – than the rights accorded every other citizen.

But we can make it so by daring to dream of a world in which we are free. So, if you dream of a world in which you can put your partner's picture on your desk, then put his picture on your desk and you will live in such a world.

And if you dream of a world in which you can hold your lover's hand when walking down the street, then hold her hand and you will live in such a world.

And if you dream of a world in which there are more openly gay elected officials, then run for office and you will live in such a world.

...if you dream of a world in which you can hold your lover's hand when walking down the street, then hold her hand and you will live in such a world.

_____

Tammy Baldwin

JUSTICE MICHAEL KIRBY

Australian Judge and Academic
b. 1939

There Will Be No U-Turns

Opening Ceremony of Gay Games VI,
Sydney, Australia

2nd November 2002

Justice Michael Kirby remains one of the most powerful openly gay men in the Australian justice system; having served as a High Court judge for thirteen years, he retired in 2009, but has remained an active voice, particularly on human rights issues. He has had a partner of nearly fifty years in Johan van Vloten and has been an openly gay public figure since 1984, just six years after the first gay riots in Sydney – an event better known today as Sydney Mardi Gras. Kirby has often spoken and advocated for gay rights, and within the law he has used his position to lobby for more consideration of human rights for the queer community.

His skill as an orator and a public speaker can be seen from this excerpt of his speech at the opening of the 2002 Gay Games VI in Sydney. Kirby gave the speech in front of a crowd of 35,000 people, telling them that the fight goes on, and with the hopeful message that the movement towards equality is unstoppable.

Under different stars, at the beginning of a new millennium, in an old land and a young nation, we join together in the hope and conviction that the future will be kinder and more just than the past....

This is a great night for Australia because we are a nation in the process of reinventing ourselves. We began our modern history by denying the existence of our Indigenous peoples and their rights. We embraced White Australia. Women could play little part in public life: their place was in the kitchen. And as for gays, lesbians and other sexual minorities, they were an abomination ... We have not corrected all these wrongs. But we are surely on the road to enlightenment. There will be no U-turns.

The changes over thirty years would not have happened if it had not been for people of courage who rejected the common ignorance about sexuality. Who taught that variations are a normal and universal aspect of the human species. That they are not going away....

Let the word go out from Sydney and the Gay Games of 2002 that the movement for equality is unstoppable ... Be sure that, in the end, inclusion will replace exclusion. For the sake of the planet and of humanity it must be so. Enjoy yourselves. And by our lives let us be an example of respect for human rights. Not just for gays. For everyone.

EVAN WOLFSON

American Attorney and Gay Marriage Advocate
b. 1957

Evan Wolfson is considered by many to be a founding member of the gay marriage movement. From his university thesis onwards he developed the legal arguments that would underpin the movement. He was also passionate about using the language of marriage and adopting the cultural signifiers as part of the whole process. 'One of the main protections that come with marriage is the word "marriage". It brings clarity.... It's a statement that you're sharing your life with someone. No one ever wrote a song about civil union'.

In this speech he speaks to the parallels between the black civil rights movement of the 1960s and the struggle facing the LGBTQ+ community in the early 2000s. Marriage is one of the cornerstones of what we consider to be heteronormative power structure – also maintained by a default belief in the binary gender model and gender roles. Marriage is the one aspect of queer theory where LGBTQ+ people faced clear discrimination and could achieve equality by legal means rather than culture change. Whether or not queer people want anything to do with heteronormative notions of monogamous lifelong relationships then becomes a matter of personal choice.

Marriage Equality and Lessons for the Scary Work of Winning

NLGLA, Lavender Law Conference, Minneapolis, Minnesota, USA

30th September 2004

America is again in a civil rights moment, as same-sex couples, their loved ones, and non-gay allies struggle to end discrimination in marriage.... Today it is gay people, same-sex couples, LGBT individuals and their loved ones and non-gay allies ... who are contesting second-class citizenship, fighting for our loved ones and our country, seeking inclusion and equality – and it is scary as well as thrilling to see the changes and feel the movement.

How can we get through this moment of peril and secure the promise?

There are lessons we can learn from those who went before us ... for we are not the first to have to fight for equality and inclusion. In fact, we are not the first to have to challenge discrimination even in marriage.

You see, marriage has always been a human rights battleground on which our nation has grappled with larger questions about what kind of country we are going to be....

Why is it so important that we now all redouble our outreach, our voices, our conversations in the vocabulary of marriage equality?

In part, because victory is within reach. In part, because we can and must move that middle now to make room for that generational momentum and rise to fairness. In part, because America is listening and allies are increasing. In part, because this is our moment of greatest peril. And, in part, because the stakes are so great.

What is at stake in this civil rights and human rights moment? ...

... If this struggle for same-sex couples' freedom to marry were 'just' about gay people, it would be important, but it is not 'just' about gay people....

... If this struggle were 'just' about marriage, it would be important, but it is not 'just' about marriage.

What is at stake in this struggle is what kind of country we are going to be....

All of us, gay and non-gay, who share the visions of America as a nation that believes that all people have the right to be both different and equal, and that without real and sufficient justification, government may not compel people to give up their difference in order to be treated equally....

What is at stake in this struggle is what kind of country we are going to be...

Evan Wolfson

PAUL MARTIN

Canadian Prime Minister (2003–06)
b. 1938

The fight for equality should end in equality. Equal opportunity for all. For that to happen any community will need to cultivate and hear words of alliance from every side, including those who may have previously opposed them. It is why demonstrations must eventually give way to discourse and democracy. Paul Martin's political legacy is unlikely to be defined by his 'volte-face' on same-sex marriage, but he was prime minister when the issue came to a head in Canada and his speech to support the bill in February 2005 made a clear case for the importance of marriage in the move towards equality.

Despite opposing the motion when it was originally raised in 1999, Martin changed his stance in 2004. Like most people who open their minds to think about this topic, he came to understand that marriage is one of the core pillars of normative exclusion: if we cannot be married, then we cannot be normal. In this light, marriage becomes about human rights rather than religious doctrine. In this speech, Paul Martin makes the case that equality is an absolute; you cannot have shades of equality. As he said: 'We embrace freedom and equality in theory. We must also embrace them in fact.... Put simply, we must always remember that "separate but equal" is not equal'.

When Martin made his speech, it made Canada only the fourth country in the world to legalize marriage between partners regardless of gender.

Bill C-38 (The Civil Marriage Act)

House of Commons, Ottawa, Canada
16th February 2005

Mr. Speaker, I rise today in support of Bill C-38, the civil marriage act. I rise in support of a Canada in which liberties are safeguarded, rights are protected and the people of this land are treated as equals under the law.

... Our deliberations will not be merely about a piece of legislation or sections of legal text. More deeply they will be about the kind of nation we are today and the nation we want to be.

... Ultimately, there is only one issue before the House in this debate. For most Canadians, in most parts of our country, same-sex marriage is already the law of the land. Thus, the issue is not whether rights are to be granted. The issue is whether rights that have been granted are to be taken away.

... Over time, perspectives changed. We evolved and we grew and our laws evolved and grew with us. That is as it should be. Our laws must reflect equality, not as we understood it a century or even a decade ago, but as we understand it today.

... Four years ago I stood in the House and voted to support the traditional definition of marriage. Many of us did. My misgivings about extending the right of civil marriage to same-sex couples were a function of my faith and my perspective on the world around us, but much has changed since that day.

... I urge those who would oppose the bill to consider that the core of the issue before us today is whether the rights of all Canadians are to be respected. I believe they must be: justice demands it, fairness demands it and the Canada we love demands it.

... The people of Canada have worked hard to build a country that opens its doors to include all, regardless of their differences; a country that respects all, regardless of their differences; and a country that demands equality for all, regardless of their differences. If we do not step forward, then we will step back. If we do not protect a right, then we deny it. Together as a nation, together as Canadians, let us step forward.

Our laws must reflect equality, not as we understood it a century or even a decade ago, but as we understand it today.

Paul Martin

IAN HUNTER

Australian Politician
b. 1960

Australian politics has an ugly, jeering, uncouth misogyny to
its daily proceedings that can be uncomfortable to watch.
Not to mention the actual politics. But it also has something
remarkable: it has a habit of producing speeches with all
the rigour of parliamentary debate, combined with a rawness
and personal flavour that would be unthinkable in larger
Western democracies.

   In this speech by Ian Hunter, the well-trodden arguments
in favour of gay marriage are rehearsed with a poignancy that
is impossible to resist. 'I rise today to speak about a matter
close to my heart. I want to get married,' he begins, 'but I
can't – I can't marry the person I love; not in my own country
at least'. The speech contains the usual barracking of the
government's demagoguery and the villainy of then prime
minister, Kevin Rudd, before it turns, and begins to hit the
personal tone that sent the speech viral on social networks.
At that point, the speech stopped being by a politician and
began to be a personal perspective that we rarely hear – a
man who proudly loved another man, and had done for many
years. Sadly, it would be another decade before the Australian
parliament would be forced by plebisicite to legalize gay
marriage. Leith and Ian did get married, in 2012, in Spain.

**No-one has ever
been able to provide
me with an adequate
response as to why
marriage should be
confined to a man
and a woman.**

———————————

Ian Hunter

A Matter of Interest

New Parliament House, Canberra, Australia

17th June 2009

I no longer think that it is adequate that I might one day be able to go to the local council and register my partnership as I might register my dog. I want to get married.

Around the world, the fight for marriage equality has been going on – and around the world, states, courts, community and parliaments have been rising to the fight....

I want to get married. Next year will be the twentieth anniversary of my not-being-married to my partner, Leith....

No one has ever been able to provide me with an adequate response as to why marriage should be confined to a man and a woman. The response that this form of 'traditional marriage' should be retained because of the biblical tradition doesn't hold much water for all of us [60 per cent] who have no interest in getting married in a church....

The ability to bear and raise children is another reason often given for standing against gay marriage. You know what? I know plenty of gay parents who are wonderful parents; and I know plenty of straight couples who don't have children, either through choice or circumstance. So that doesn't hold up either....

As for the sanctity of marriage being threatened by gay marriage – all I can say to that is: if your heterosexual marriage is going to be somehow devalued by your homosexual neighbours' marriage, that says more about your relationship than it does about mine.

The marriage equality debate is gathering speed around the world and yet Australia finds itself once again a backwater in this debate. It is time for the community's voice to be raised, calling for marriage equality and I add my voice to that call today.

Because I want to get married – and you, Mr Rudd, are stopping me.

DAN SAVAGE & TERRY MILLER

American Relationship and Sex Advice Columnist and Pundit, and Terry Miller, Founders of the 'It Gets Better' Project
b. 1964 & b. 1971

To older readers, Dan Savage will forever be synonymous with 'Savage Love', the sex advice column that he wrote through the 1990s that offered light into the darkness of closeted queer lives in an era before the internet. Savage can be thanked for neologisms such as 'pegging', 'saddleback', and 'monogamish'. Savage represented an enlightened, funny, sexy community that I felt I could never be part of.

In September 2010, shocked by a number of suicides of queer teens that appeared to be related to bullying around sexual identity, Savage and his husband, Terry Miller, decided to make their own video trying to reach out to those kids they couldn't meet in person, and tell them it would be alright, that life would get better; that school was just a phase; that older gay adults were living happy, productive, love-filled lives and that they were looking forward to meeting them. It provoked an astonishing outpouring from all around the world.

As they would soon write on the 'It Gets Better' website created to house the hundreds – and eventually tens of thousands – of videos that flooded in: 'Many LGBT youths can't picture what their lives might be like as openly gay adults. They can't imagine a future for themselves. So let's show them what our lives are like, let's show them what the future may hold in store for them'.

It Gets Better

YouTube.com, USA

21st September 2010

TM: My school was pretty miserable. I lived in Spokane, WA, which is a mid-size town with a small-town mentality. And I was picked on mercilessly in school; people were really cruel to me. I was bullied a lot, beat up, thrown against walls and lockers and windows. You know, stuffed into bathroom stalls, people shit on my car, people scratched my car, broke my windows. And my parents went in once to talk to the school administrators about the harassment I was getting in school, and they basically said, 'If you look that way, walk that way, talk that way, act that way, then there's nothing we can do to help your son.'

... Honestly, things got better the day I left high school. I didn't see the bullies every day, I didn't see the people who harassed me every day, I didn't have to see the school administrators who would do nothing about it every day. Life instantly got better.

DS: If there are 14-, 15-, 16-year olds ... 13-year olds, 12-year olds out there watching this video, what I'd love you to take away from it really is that IT GETS BETTER. However bad it is now, it gets better. And it can get great and it can get awesome. Your life can be amazing, but you have to tough this period ahead out and you have to live your life so that you're around for it to get amazing. And it can, and it will.

... When I first came out to my folks, they weren't thrilled. My mother said she never wanted to meet any of my boyfriends. And I was never to bring a man around that I was dating to the house. Ever. My mother recently passed away, and she told me to let Terry know that she loved him like a daughter. And she did! She loved you like you were my spouse.

TM: She did.

DS: And you were welcome in the house and our families are really accepting. You would think, my Evangelical Catholic parents, Terry's conservative Christian parents who sent him to that awful school, that our families would reject us forever and never get over it. Wouldn't embrace us. But both of our families, Terry's family ... and my family love us, and accept us and include us.

However bad it is now,
it gets better.
And it can get great
and it can get awesome.

_____

Dan Savage & Terry Miller

ARSHAM PARSI

Iranian LGBTQ+ Rights Activist and Director of the Marjan Foundation
b. 1981

A Letter to a Beloved Friend

Lethbridge Community Celebrating Diversity Conference, Alberta, Canada
6th October 2010

In his speech in Alberta in 2010, Arsham Parsi approached the lectern and seemed to consider whether to acknowledge the warm and kind introduction he had just received ahead of his address to the attendees of the Lethbridge Community Celebrating Diversity Conference.
He dithered and then started abruptly: 'I do not recall when you committed suicide. I cannot remember the exact date that I came to your room and saw those bloody sheets of yours.'

Arsham Parsi is a remarkable man with a life dedicated to challenging the Iranian government's systematic oppression of LGBTQ+ people. Firstly, through the clandestine queer chat network he set up during his time in Iran and more recently, through his organization, the Iranian Railroad for Queer Refugees, which helps queer individuals escape persecution from their home countries. He himself was a refugee and in this speech he recounts his history in an evocative and painful letter to his friend. Explaining how he has been inspired to help queer Iranian refugees access 'friendly' and 'tolerant' Western countries, he also laments his loss of his friend who could not escape when his sexuality was discovered.

'I miss you a lot and I would like to write this letter to you.... Our friendship did not last long before you decided to take your life after your mother saw you in your bed with your boyfriend. I cannot forgive you for not locking your door.'

You know that I too have a dream, my dream is that one day the rights of all queers be recognized and be respected everywhere. That one day no one will be executed, tortured, arrested, imprisoned, isolated or disowned by their families and communities merely for the crime of being queer. I dream of the day when my and other innocent Iranians' sexual orientation will not be legal cause to deprive us of our fundamental human rights, that is the day that no one commits suicide on the basis of their sexual orientation like you did, my dearly departed friend. That is my dream and greatest wish for myself and for all the voiceless in Iran who cannot speak for themselves ... They cannot speak their conscience in today's Islamic Republic of Iran without fear of terrible reprisal from the authorities, so I must speak out on their behalf. My own conscience dedicates to know this, I declare this dream of mine for ours. I will repeat it loudly and often and hope one day soon to achieve this dream for all of my fellow citizens in [the] Iran that I love and once called home ... Iran is not merely where I am from, it is who I am. Again, I miss you and you will be remembered forever. I'm fond of the month of October, seems it has been [a time that we] achieve a lot, especially 6th October. I would like to name today after you, the memorial day for all Iranian queers who are not with us today.

RABBI SHARON KLEINBAUM

American Rabbi and LGBTQ+ Advocate
b. 1959

Sharon Kleinbaum is the Senior Rabbi at Congregation
Beit Simchat Torah in New York City. In 2010, she filmed a
wonderful open statement to children of all faiths and all
orientations in which she describes herself very simply:
'I am a lesbian'. And that is the tone of the speech as a whole.
It is disarming partly because it is so frank and sincere;
there is an absence of guile and no apparent agenda. She
even ends by welcoming bullies to contact her. This does
slightly date the film to early era internet but it is nonetheless
charming and bold.

   This speech is an early indicator of how the internet was
taken up by the LGBTQ+ community and used as a medium
to reach out to the fringes – especially the youth – and build a
communication network that has enabled significant progress
over the last twenty years. Prior to sites like YouTube, there
was no obvious way for Rabbi Kleinbaum to share her lived
experience beyond her local community; no way for a Jewish
lesbian rabbi in New York to talk to gay youth in Tel Aviv or
Glasgow or Bucharest. The internet opened up an avenue for
local pastors and community leaders to reach out and share
their support all over the world.

A Word to the Bullies

New York City, New York
25th October 2010

There are those who say that God hates gays. There are those who say that Hashem has given us all challenges and your challenge is to overcome your feelings: either be celibate for the rest of your life or be with opposite sex partners. There are those who say we are either criminal or sick or sinful. None of these are true – we are all created in God's image. All genders, all sexual orientations, all races, all sizes, all of us.

All different types of kids are bullied but the bullying is the same. Cowards ... take it out on those of us who are different: smaller, smarter, differently abled, immigrants, gay-looking kids, girls who aren't cheerleader types, kids with accents, kids with two moms [or] two dads, kids with a mentally ill parent....

I know this message might not be enough. When I was younger and living in the closet I thought I was the only living lesbian on the planet. I went to a psychiatrist to make me straight. We've come a long way since ... and we still have so far to go. If you are feeling this kind of hurt, I ask you to hold on. You are not alone. You are sacred and you are beautiful and there are people who care about you. I am one of them.

... We may not be in the same state or even in the same country but we care about you and there are communities and people like ours all over the world.

... A word to the bullies out there. I know that most people who bully others for being gay or looking gay are often struggling with their own feelings.... Contact me to talk and if you don't agree, contact me to bully me. I'm a lesbian and I'd rather you bully me than a thirteen-year-old kid.

... We are all created in God's image. Now let's live up to it.

...We may not be in the same state or even in the same country but we care about you and there are communities and people like ours all over the world.

—————————

Rabbi Sharon Kleinbaum

HILLARY RODHAM CLINTON

First Lady of the United States (1993–2001), US Senator for New York
(2001–09), US Secretary of State (2009–13)
b. 1947

Hillary Rodham Clinton is not a name that requires a long
introduction. After losing an astonishing presidential race to Donald
Trump in 2016, she was one of the most famous people in the world.
Before that, however, she had a long and distinguished career as a
lawyer and as a diplomat, both as First Lady of the United States and
as Secretary of State.

   Throughout her career Clinton always focused on gender equality,
like many politicians. However, her view on marriage equality
evolved more slowly – a fact she acknowledges in this lecture that
she gave to a United Nation audience in Geneva in 2011. Speaking
on International Human Rights Day, she spoke passionately about
the needs of LGBTQ+ folk, demolishing many commonly held
falsehoods and hammering home our fundamental human rights.
The Washington Post called the speech 'blunt yet inspiring' and
the audience gave it a standing ovation. Her words took many by
surprise because of the absolute and unequivocal way it was sent as
a message to the world: the United States believed, as she did, that
'being LGBTQ+ does not make you less human. And that is why gay
rights are human rights, and human rights are gay rights'.

All people deserve to be treated with dignity and have their human rights respected, no matter who they are or whom they love.

Hillary Rodham Clinton

International Human Rights Day Address

Geneva, Switzerland

6th December 2011

Today, I want to talk about the work we have left to do to protect one group of people whose human rights are still denied in too many parts of the world today. In many ways, they are an invisible minority. They are arrested, beaten, terrorized, even executed. Many are treated with contempt and violence by their fellow citizens while authorities empowered to protect them look the other way or, too often, even join in the abuse. They are denied opportunities to work and learn, driven from their homes and countries, and forced to suppress or deny who they are to protect themselves from harm.

... It is a violation of human rights when people are beaten or killed because of their sexual orientation, or because they do not conform to cultural norms about how men and women should look or behave. It is a violation of human rights when governments declare it illegal to be gay, or allow those who harm gay people

to go unpunished. It is a violation of human rights when lesbian or transgendered women are subjected to so-called corrective rape, or forcibly subjected to hormone treatments, or when people are murdered after public calls for violence toward gays, or when they are forced to flee their nations and seek asylum in other lands to save their lives....

There is little doubt in my mind that support for LGBT human rights will continue to climb. Because for many young people, this is simple: All people deserve to be treated with dignity and have their human rights respected, no matter who they are or whom they love.

... Those who advocate for expanding the circle of human rights were and are on the right side of history, and history honors them. Those who tried to constrict human rights were wrong, and history reflects that as well.

ANNA GRODZKA

Poland's First Transgender MP (2011–15)
b. 1954

Poland has a poor standing within the European Union when it comes to LGBTQ+ rights. However, in 2011 Anna Grodzka's election to the Polish Parliament marked only the third time a transgender woman had been elected to a national parliament anywhere in the world after Georgina Beyer (in New Zealand) and Vladimir Luxuria (in Italy). Grodzka served as a member of the Green Party and was the party's candidate for president in 2015. She generated unexpected amounts of goodwill in her campaigning but also enormous vitriol and opposition. On one occasion another Polish MP, Krystyna Pawłowicz, called her out in a public meeting, stating that she looked like a professional boxer and that she had 'no right to even be in a public space'.

Grodzka's time in office was marked by tension around marriage equality, civil partnerships and other LGBTQ+ rights issues in Poland, a conservative Catholic country. Her very presence in parliament and her refusal to define her sexuality within a binary spectrum made her a beacon in the more liberal sectors of Polish society. In her speech given on the International Day Against Homophobia, Biphobia and Transphobia [IDAHOBIT] in 2013, she spoke of the absence of LGBTQ+ rights in so many countries, including Poland, the right to equality and of acceptance.

Kaleidoscope Trust Annual IDAHOT Lecture

The Commonwealth Club, London, UK

17th May 2013

In my country school curricula do not include the topic of homosexuality. Same-sex partnerships are not regulated by law, and homophobic hate speech is present everywhere: in the media, in churches, in the streets and even in the parliament....

It's been almost two years since a [political] breakthrough which triggered a process of change in Poland.... Together ... the first openly gay MP and I were elected. Our party demands the adoption of civil partnerships bill, gender recognition act, a bill safeguarding equal rights and opportunities for women in the labour market, prohibition of hate speech and the introduction of anti-discriminatory laws....

There is much said about the need for tolerance of non-heterosexual people. I do not demand tolerance, I demand equal rights. I demand acceptance for every human being who does not do any harm with his actions to anyone else. I demand acceptance for every human being because it should be the right of all persons. I demand acceptance for human diversity because it is the humanistic responsibility of all people....

The experience of transsexuality brings us to two important conclusions.

Transsexual behaviour cannot be considered a deviation but behaviour that displays the real nature of a human being. A human being understood as a social construct which can encompass various forms of self-identification. In other words, the experiences of transsexual people teach us what a human being really is.... We have the right to our own gender, our own psycho-sexual orientation in the same ways as we have the right to our beliefs, our integrity and dignity.

... Unfortunately ... this is not shared by everybody. The mighty Catholic Church in Poland denies transsexual people the right to gender that is congruent with their feeling and calls the bodily sex adjustment to gender identity an act of mutilation.

... Those who have the only righteous vision of what a human being should be, need to be reminded that the natural characteristic of nature is diversity, a natural feature of society is fairness and the natural feature of a person is humanism.

... I believe that also, thanks to you, the world will become a better, fairer place.

Transsexual behaviour cannot be considered a deviation but behaviour that displays the real nature of a human being...

———————

Anna Grodzka

GEORGE TAKEI

American Actor, Director, Author and Activist
b. 1937

George Takei is an icon, not just to *Star Trek* fans – for whom he is forever remembered as Commander Sulu – but for a generation of queer people who have grown up online and enjoyed his humour, his ability to listen, and his repeated stands against homophobia from elected officials. As with many twentieth-century Hollywood stars, Takei only felt able to publicly acknowledge that he was gay in 2005, despite his well-known relationship of over eighteen years with Brad Altman, whom he later married.

Takei has enjoyed a long career as an actor and director, and as a political activist both for LGBTQ+ and Japanese-American causes. Known for hot takes and inflammatory comments, Takei is a natural fit for the fast wit and short fuse of the internet, where he has found his second home on Facebook and Twitter. In May 2014, the Gay and Lesbian Alliance Against Defamation honoured Takei with the GLAAD Vito Russo Award, which is presented to public figures making a significant difference in the promotion of equality for the LGBTQ+ community. In his acceptance speech, Takei focused on the importance of visibility by prominent queer people and stressed how far there was still to go.

GLAAD Acceptance Award

New York City, New York, USA
12th April 2014

As a closeted kid growing up in Los Angeles ... all I saw of gay[s] and lesbians in movies and television or heard on the radio were caricatures of people who were mocked and laughed at, or pitied, or hated. The media stripped us of all humanity and made us into pathetic stereotypes. The media then was a soul-crushing monster. GLAAD took on this formidable beast with its media-savvy, political acumen and the power of its advocacy and transformed the media into a powerful force for change. GLAAD inspired and galvanized others into action to join in with the great twenty-first century civil rights movement....

But as long as LGBT people can be fired from their jobs for simply being who they are, our work isn't done. As long as young people are kicked out of their families just for being who they are, our work is not done. As long as people are being bullied into feeling that their lives are so hopeless that they are driven to self-destructive acts, our work is not done. Working in concert with GLAAD, with its history of achievement and the legacy of Vito Russo, we will make this a better world, a more equal society of all people....

DEBI JACKSON

American Mother, Trans Advocate and Founder of Gender Inc.
b. 1974

The best parents are supportive parents. When Debi
Jackson stood up to defend the validity of her child she was
the best kind of supportive. Enabling, validating, supportive
and fierce. Debi said that she had never even heard the word
'transgender' before her four-year-old daughter (assigned male
at birth) told her, 'Mom, you know I'm really a girl, right? I'm a
girl on the inside'. Debi let her daughter go to school in girl
clothes, and was delighted to see her child finally happy in
herself, surrounded by supportive kids and teachers. 'But then
the kids went home, and told their parents and they weren't
so great after that'. After being hounded and her daughter
being outed as trans in the press, Jackson came out and gave
a typically robust response. 'I'm the mom of the little girl
called A.J. who was recently profiled in the *Kansas City Star*.
As surprised as I was to find my family in the paper I'm also
incredibly proud,' she began. And through her speech she
began to unpick, argument by argument, the assumptions and
criticisms that the parents of trans kids are regularly exposed
to in Western society.

That's Good Enough

Unity Temple, Kansas City, Kansas, USA
3rd May 2014

When I tell our daughter's story, I hear the same uninformed comments over and over again, so I'd like to address a few of those now.

1. We are liberals pushing a gay agenda. Nope, sorry. I'm a conservative Southern Baptist Republican from Alabama.

2. We ... wanted a girl so we turned our child into one. Again no. I desperately wanted boys. The idea of raising a girl in today's world scares me to death.

3. 'Kids have no idea what they want or who they are. My kid wants to be a dog, should I let him?' That's up to you but I wouldn't. There is a profound difference between wanting to be something in imaginary play and in declaring who you are insistently, consistently, and persistently....

4. Kids shouldn't have to learn about sex at such a young age. Well, I agree so it's a good thing that being transgender has nothing to do with sex!

5. Transgender people are perverts and shouldn't be in the bathroom with 'normal' people. I don't know what you go into a bathroom to do but I know what my daughter goes in there for... and it isn't to look around. It's to ... pee where no one else can see her.

6. God hates transgender people. They are sinners and going to Hell.... Some people choose to embrace biblical verses that appear to say being transgender is wrong. I choose to focus on verses like 1st Samuel 16:7 which says, 'But the Lord said to Samuel, "Do not consider his appearance or his height, for I have rejected him. The Lord does not look at the things people look at. People look at the outward appearance, but the Lord looks at the heart."'

My daughter is a girl in her heart. She knows it. God knows it. And that's good enough for me.

My daughter is a girl in her heart. She knows it. God knows it. And that's good enough for me.

Debi Jackson

JÓHANNA SIGURÐARDÓTTIR

Politician and Former Prime Minister of Iceland (2009–12)
b. 1942

Jóhanna Sigurðardóttir met her future wife in the mid-1980s. In 2009 she was elected Prime Minister of Iceland, a post she retained until 2012 when she stepped down from politics. She was the world's first openly gay prime minister and became one of Iceland's most recognizable politicians.

Many of us grew up in a time when a country having an openly gay, female prime minister seemed completely unthinkable. The battle is never over, and the impossible is never impossible. The decade since Sigurðardóttir left office has been one of turbo-charged perception shift, helped in no small amount by such visible role models.

Sigurðardóttir's speech to WorldPride in 2014 has additional pathos when considered in the context of her relationship with her partner Jónína Leósdóttir. Both were married with children, and without any sense of being 'gay' the pair slowly fell in love and eventually divorced their husbands. Leósdóttir has talked of how scared they both were for their families and their careers, especially Sigurðardóttir's political future. Consequently, they lived apart, in a secret relationship, for almost fifteen years, before finally moving in together in 2000 and marrying in 2010. It is a story that many of that older generation understand, and seems inexplicable to the youngest generation. One can only hope that a life spent in secret remains unthinkable.

Sigurðardóttir spoke of the plight of many gay people around the world for whom life must still be conducted in secret. She asked if we have done enough to support our community in countries where human rights are still abused.

Love is simply love.

Jóhanna Sigurðardóttir

WorldPride Human Rights Conference 2014 Address

Toronto, Ontario, Canada

25th June 2014

I freely confess, here at my first WorldPride Conference, that when I look in life's rear-view mirror I see that we [Sigurðardóttir and Leósdóttir] did not need to wait for so long to be open about our feelings. The attitude in Iceland [became] much more accepting long before the year 2000 when we finally started living together....

My heart is full of gratitude ... and I am grateful to all of you who are gathered here today. I am sure that many of you have had a long and difficult fight for gay rights....

The story of my and Jónína's love is certainly a tale of struggle. It is full of strong emotions and great conflict, accusation, guilt and great worries.... And the endless fear of what could happen in the ruthless world of politics. But our story is also a tale of triumph, because in the end love conquered all.

... Therefore Jónína and I have reason to be thankful. Our time did come at last. But our joy is mixed with sadness. It is difficult to enjoy a life of freedom and tolerance while thousands of our brothers and sisters in other countries have to fear for their lives every single day....

It is vitally important that every human being's freedom and human rights are respected all over the world. Freedom and human rights – that is what the world needs most, and what every individual longs for ... freedom and human rights ensures that everyone can live with dignity.... No one should have to endure oppression, abuse ... or ... forfeit their life for the fundamental human right of living in accord with their feelings....

It is terrible that in 2014 there are still eighty-three countries in the world with some kind of anti-gay laws and that in some of these places these laws are ruthlessly enforced.... It is terrible that in up to ten countries it is a capital offence to be gay and that there are laws that sentence queer people to death by public stoning.

... Ladies and Gentlemen, leaders of nations where freedom and human rights are respected must not let this carry on. They have to unite.... They have to take action against states that cruelly disregard the human rights of queer people.... And the question is, don't these hundreds of millions of people deserve that the global community stands united in the fight for their freedom and human rights? Of course they do!...

More has to be done. Much more.... The fight for queer equal rights is not over until the whole world – the whole world – understands that the feelings of gays, lesbians, bisexual and transgender people are exactly the same as the feelings of heterosexuals. Love is simply love.

LEE MOKOBE

South African Activist and Poet
b. 1996

While it is important to have powerful allies that will stand up on behalf of queer people, often the best words – and the most valid and the most powerful words – come from the lived experience of queer people themselves. In 2015, Lee Mokobe, a nineteen-year-old from Cape Town, captured what is, for the huge majority of people, an unthinkable phenomenon. Speaking at the TED Women conference in California he performed a poem which speaks of what it is like to be transgender.

This speech is a powerful example of the process of eloquently communicating to someone who can never understand how you feel. Yes, you can read his words here, but you also have permission to turn to your phone and watch him on YouTube. He performs the words and speaks so beautifully about profound truths and the practical nightmares of growing up trans in a world that does not want transgender people to even exist. Mokobe is an inspiration to young activists anywhere that their voices are valid and their experience can influence millions of people when they find the courage to speak their truth.

What it Feels Like to be Transgender

Monterey, California

May 2015

... My mother told me of the miracle I was, said I could grow up to be anything I want. I decided to be a boy.

... I was the mystery of an anatomy, a question asked but not answered, tightroping between awkward boy and apologetic girl, and when I turned 12, the boy phase wasn't deemed cute anymore. It was met with nostalgic aunts who missed seeing my knees in the shadow of skirts, who reminded me that my kind of attitude would never bring a husband home, that I exist for heterosexual marriage and child-bearing. And I swallowed their insults along with their slurs.

Naturally, I did not come out of the closet. The kids at my school opened it without my permission. Called me by a name I did not recognize, said 'lesbian', but I was more boy than girl, more Ken than Barbie.

... No one ever thinks of us as human because we are more ghost than flesh, because people fear that my gender expression is a trick, that it exists to be perverse, that it ensnares them without their consent, that my body is a feast for their eyes and hands and once they have fed off my queer, they'll regurgitate all the parts they did not like.

... Can you see how easy it is to talk people into coffins, to misspell their names on gravestones. And people still wonder why there are boys rotting, they go away in high school hallways, they are afraid of becoming another hashtag in a second, afraid of classroom discussions becoming like judgement day and now oncoming traffic is embracing more transgender children than parents.

I wonder how long it will be before the trans suicide notes start to feel redundant, before we realize that our bodies become lessons about sin way before we learn how to love them.

My mother...said I could grow up to be anything I want. I decided to be a boy

---

Lee Mokobe

ALISON BECHDEL

American Comic Book Artist
b. 1960

Alison Bechdel is a brilliant comic book artist who will always be associated with 'The Bechdel Test', a formula for illustrating the representation of women in film. The 'test' was first published in her 1985 comic strip called 'The Rule', one of a long-running series called Dykes to Watch Out For [DTWOF], which brought an understanding of lesbian culture to a global audience. Fascinatingly, when re-read today, over thirty years later, it is not only still laugh-out-loud funny and scarily accurate, but it also mirrors the sense of crisis and impending existential disaster that overwhelms so many of us. Bechdel's strips have a visionary genius.

Today in a time of legal equity and marriage equality, some queer folk can imagine themselves 'free' in a world that is relatively harmless to them. For Bechdel and older generations, the realization that this milestone had been reached came along with another awareness – the knowledge that they had been assimilated into mainstream contemporary culture. Being 'accepted' had meant the loss of communal identity that came from being 'other'. As Krista Burton captured so perfectly for her *New York Times* Op-Ed: 'Hipster style is just queer style, particularly queer women's style. Put another way: lesbians invented hipsters'.

Bechdel speaks to both the melancholy and the magic of this identity crisis. Spanning the genesis of her work and inspiration, her CUNY speech was a comedic duet between her words and chosen cartoons from her history, but it also worked well in transcript. In it, Bechdel began to pick apart her changing role from outlaw to in-law and created a cat's cradle of what it means to be queer in a world where her sexuality is normal.

Queers and Comics

City University of New York (CUNY), New York City, USA

8th May 2015

Okay, so, queers and comics – who knew back in the early 1980s that becoming a lesbian cartoonist would actually, like, be a good career move? [laughter]

… [T]here's been a very interesting parallel trajectory between these realms [LGBT and comics] over the past three or four decades. There has been this movement in both cases from the shadows into the light from the under-ground into the mainstream, from a belief that both gay people and comics are child molesters, to a world where not only can gay people get married, gay cartoon characters can get married….

In 1980 there was this very separate subculture for gay people where queerness was not just okay but, like, revolutionary. I felt then like I didn't want or need approval from the broader culture. I felt like mainstream culture was kind of irrelevant to my concerns. But gradually that started to change for everyone….

I guess I had always hoped that we were gonna change the world, not that we would get assimilated into the world – but both of those things happened, both of those operations were at work. My goal with my work has changed over the years. My original mission was to prove that dykes were okay – and I feel like there's been a lot of progress to that end – but then I started to want something else. I wanted my comic strip to make the leap from being 'a lesbian comic strip' to being 'just a comic strip'. Occasionally a straight person or a reviewer would say that my work was 'universal' and I love that adjective, it was sort of cool, but it also bugged me because behind that word 'universal' I can't help but sense this lurking fear of difference. It's conditional approval and I want an unconditional approval. I wanted to be okay even if I wasn't like you – that's why I never tried to explain or defend lesbianism in my comic….

As much as I love being a big queer, as much as I love drawing comics, I find myself thinking about what would it mean to not need these categories? What if there was no LGBT studies shelf? What if there was no comics shelf?… What would it mean for comics to be just another way of telling a story and for queerness to be just another way of relating to people? In a way it's a scary thought. I don't really want to let go of these tethers – a world without categories would be kind of overwhelm-ing and impossible – but still … I think it's something worth thinking about.

As much as I love being a big queer, as much as I love drawing comics, I find myself thinking about what would it mean to not need these categories?

_____

Alison Bechdel

BARACK OBAMA

44th President of the United States (2009–17)
b. 1961

Barack Obama was the first African American to be elected to the presidency of the United States, serving from 2009 to 2017. His political career grew through his work for the Democratic Party in Chicago, often focused on registering voters. An early opponent of the Iraq War, he was awarded the Nobel Peace Prize in 2009. He led America and the world through the global financial crisis that began in 2009, and most notably passed the Affordable Care Act in 2010 to reduce the number of Americans who did not have health cover.

Interestingly, on the subject of marriage Obama appeared to move from supporting it (in 1996), to being opposed to it, to supporting it again. In 2012 he described himself as 'going through an evolution on this issue'. The truth of this, as for all politicians, is that their beliefs are malleable. And this is okay. Successful politicians hold up a mirror to the shifting beliefs of society and cultural currents, and therefore in changing their minds reflect the changes in wider society. In 2015 the United States was finally ready for same-sex marriage, and Obama's administration was able to press for that change. When the Supreme Court made its judgement, we were fortunate to have a remarkable orator in the White House to elegantly commemorate the day.

Supreme Court Ruling on Same-Sex Marriage

Washington, D.C., USA

26th June 2015

I know change for many of our LGBT brothers and sisters must have seemed so slow for so long. But compared to so many other issues, America's shift has been so quick ...

We are big and vast and diverse; a nation of people with different backgrounds and beliefs, different experiences and stories, but bound by our shared ideal that no matter who you are or what you look like, how you started off, or how and who you love, America is a place where you can write your own destiny. We are a people who believe that every single child is entitled to life and liberty and the pursuit of happiness.

There's so much more work to be done to extend the full promise of America to every American. But today, we can say in no uncertain terms that we've made our union a little more perfect.

That's the consequence of a decision from the Supreme Court, but, more importantly, it is a consequence of the countless small acts of courage of millions of people across decades who stood up, who came out, who talked to parents – parents who loved their children no matter what. Folks who were willing to endure bullying and taunts, and stayed strong, and came to believe in themselves and who they were, and slowly made an entire country realize that love is love.

What an extraordinary achievement. What a vindication of the belief that ordinary people can do extraordinary things. What a reminder of what Bobby Kennedy once said about how small actions can be like pebbles being thrown into a still lake, and ripples of hope cascade outwards and change the world.

Those countless, often anonymous heroes – they deserve our thanks. They should be very proud. America should be very proud.

...small actions can be like pebbles being thrown into a still lake, and ripples of hope cascade outwards and change the world.

Barack Obama

SIR ELTON JOHN

British Singer, Songwriter, Composer and Producer
b. 1947

Sir Elton John is internationally famed for his singing and song-writing. Since coming out first as bisexual and then as openly gay in the 1980s, he has influenced generations of musicians, as well as raising millions for AIDS education and prevention. He is a passionate and outspoken supporter of gay marriage, and has two children with David Furnish, his partner of twenty-five years. Sir Elton may well be an icon, but the need to tell one's truth, and with dignity, spans every country and every level of society across the globe. It seems that need will never completely disappear.

For example, I did not know that Sir Elton speaks in war zones. While a convention of oligarchs and world leaders may not have been subjected to the violence that ordinary people experienced during the conflict, in 2015 he gave a powerful speech at Yalta – in recently annexed Crimea – and made the case for LGBTQ+ rights to an audience of some of the most powerful and intimidating people in the world. It requires extraordinary privilege to be afforded such a speaking platform but it is worth pausing to consider how brave and how determined one must be to speak one's truth, no matter what one's position in life.

Speech at the 12th Yalta European Strategy (YES) Annual Meeting

Yalta, Ukraine

2th September 2015

I know first-hand why many people stay in the closet. It's because of fear. Fear that they will lose their job, fear that they will lose the affection of their family and friends, fear that they may be physically assaulted either by the authorities or by their fellow citizens.

... It may be hard for you to understand that I too felt such fear. Even someone like me – a prominent and protected citizen – is not immune from fear and prejudice....

There are moments in a person's life which change everything. They are critical to one's entire future and legacy: having children, choosing sides in a war or conflict, telling the truth.

... For me, that moment was about owning up to the world about my sexual orientation. At a time when almost all gay public figures were in the closet, to publicly admit I am gay changed the way the world saw and still sees me, and changed how I felt about myself....

What has any of this to do with a conference about the future of politics, security and the economy of [the] Ukraine? Because critical moments also exist in the lives of societies and nations. The choice of freedom over repression, democracy over totalitarianism, acceptance over hatred ...

I suggest to you that your stance on human rights will also be a defining characteristic of the new Ukraine, and that there is no clearer touchstone on the issue of human rights than the respect and dignity afforded your LGBT citizens....

The people in this room are some of the most powerful in [the] Ukraine, and in some cases the most powerful anywhere in the world. You have the power to help bring about this new era. I'm asking you to use that power wisely, to seize the opportunity, and to guarantee human rights for all.

...to publicly admit I am gay changed the way the world saw and still sees me, and changed how I felt about myself...

Sir Elton John

BAN KI-MOON

*South Korean Diplomat and Secretary-General of the
United Nations (2007–16)*
b. 1944

Throughout his tenure as the eighth Secretary-General of the United
Nations, Ban Ki-moon was an outspoken advocate for LGBTQ+ rights,
as part of the UN's broader mission to secure human rights for all.
He elevated the topic to the agenda at the UN and continued to
address it throughout his tenure. In 2010 he first spoke publicly in
defence of LGBTQ+ rights as secretary-general. In 2012 he addressed
the United Nations Human Rights Council, saying: 'To those who are
lesbian, gay, bisexual or transgender, let me say: You are not alone.
Your struggle for an end to violence and discrimination is a shared
struggle. Any attack on you is an attack on the universal values of the
United Nations I have sworn to defend and uphold'. During the
speech there was an organized walk-out by a few UN representatives
in protest at his position. This echoed the opposition faced by the
earliest advocates in Germany 150 years earlier. Progress is taking
place but at a slow pace.

In his 2015 speech at the United Nations headquarters, Ban
Ki-moon spoke in a typically humble manner about his ongoing
diplomacy. Too often a politician's words are hard to gauge for
depth of sincerity, so perhaps it is better to point out that when
the secretary-general stepped down from his post in 2016 and the
Security Council sat to choose the words with which to honour him,
Russia unfortunately chose to veto the focus on his specific advocacy
for the LGBTQ+ community, instead more vaguely thanking him
for assisting 'the most vulnerable or marginalized'. The LGBTQ+
community can be grateful for his actions, and pay no mind to what
that allyship might be called.

When the human rights of LGBT people are abused, all of us are diminished. Every human life is precious – none is worth more than another.

Ban Ki-moon

Remarks at the LGBT Core Group Event: 'Leaving No one Behind: Equality and Inclusion in the Post-2015 Development Agenda'

Headquarters of the United Nations, New York City, USA

29th September 2015

In too many countries, lesbian, gay, bisexual, transgender and intersex people are among the poorest, most marginalized members of society....

Too many of our LGBT brothers and sisters are jobless, homeless and struggling to survive. The situation of transgender people is even worse overall. They have higher rates of homelessness, poverty and hunger. For individuals and their families, this is a personal tragedy. And for society, it is a shameful waste of human talent, ingenuity and economic potential....

We are here together to break down the barriers that prevent LGBT people from exercising their full human rights. When we do that, we will liberate them to fully and productively contribute to our common economic progress....

Looking at me, you would think I have very little in common with Harvey Milk. I would never claim to be as courageous as he was. But I am totally committed to this cause.

... I have been urging many world leaders whose countries have harsh domestic policies to amend them. Sometimes I am successful and other times I am not, but I will continue to fight until all LGBT people can live freely without suffering any intimidation or discrimination....

When the human rights of LGBT people are abused, all of us are diminished. Every human life is precious – none is worth more than another.

... This United Nations I lead will never shirk in the fight against discrimination. We will never shy away from protecting the most marginalized and vulnerable people. This is not just a personal commitment – it is an institutional one. Some say I am the first secretary-general to take up this cause – but I prefer to say I am the first of many....

And I say to members of the LGBT community: the United Nations will always stand with you in your fight for recognition, respect and rights.

... Let us unite for a better world for all people.

LORETTA E. LYNCH

Attorney General of the United States (2015–17)
b. 1959

Loretta E. Lynch would probably be more of a household
name if it were not for her being overshadowed by the firsts achieved
by her boss, Barack Obama. She was the very first African-American
woman to hold the position of attorney general in the United States,
and she was both the second African-American ever, and the second
woman ever, to do so. In other words, she is pretty special. If she one
day sits on the United States Supreme Court, it will be a great day for
the LGBTQ+ community, because Lynch repeatedly does what we ask
of allies: she stands up and speaks up for marginalized communities.

In 2016, Lynch provided the third great 'moment of hope' from
Obama's White House as she tore into the state of North Carolina in
a way unprecedented for a representative of a sitting US president.
The state had just legislated for a series of 'Bathroom Bills' (HB2)
directly aimed at the transgender community. It argued that that
some cisgendered people might abuse the ability to use the
bathroom of choice, and that the only way to prevent this was to
discriminate against transgender people. In order to prevent this,
Lynch filed a federal suit alleging violations of the Civil Rights Act
to strike down the law, and in her speech she unequivocally placed
transgender issues within the context of the civil rights movement
as a whole.

Denouncing North Carolina's Bathroom Law

Washington, D.C., USA

9th May 2016

This action is about a great deal more than just bathrooms. This is about the dignity and respect we accord our fellow citizens and the laws that we, as a people and as a country, have enacted to protect them – indeed, to protect all of us. And it's about the founding ideals that have led this country – haltingly but inexorably – in the direction of fairness, inclusion, and equality for all Americans.

... You've been told that this law protects vulnerable populations from harm – but that just is not the case. Instead, what this law does is inflict further indignity on a population that has already suffered far more than its fair share. This law provides no benefit to society – all it does is harm innocent Americans.

Instead of turning away from our neighbors, our friends, our colleagues, let us instead learn from our history and avoid repeating the mistakes of our past. Let us reflect on the obvious, but often neglected, lesson that state-sanctioned discrimination never looks good in hindsight. It was not so very long ago that states, including North Carolina, had signs above restrooms, water fountains, and on public accommodations keeping people out based upon a distinction without a difference. We have moved beyond those dark days, but not without pain and suffering and an ongoing fight to keep moving forward. Let us write a different story this time ...

Let me also speak directly to the transgender community itself. Some of you have lived freely for decades. Others of you are still wondering how you can possibly live the lives you were born to lead. But no matter how isolated or scared you may feel today, the Department of Justice and the entire Obama Administration wants you to know that we see you; we stand with you; and we will do everything we can to protect you going forward. Please know that history is on your side.

Instead of turning away from our neighbors, our friends, our colleagues, let us instead learn from our history and avoid repeating the mistakes of our past.

Loretta E. Lynch

GERALDINE ROMAN

Journalist and First Openly Trans Woman
Elected to Congress of the Philippines
b. 1967

First Privilege Speech Delivered by Rep. Geraldine Roman

Manila, The Philippines
19th September 2016

One's first speech as a representative of parliament must always be daunting. But for Geraldine Roman, the first openly transgender congresswoman elected to the Philippine parliament, it was both emotional and significant. The daughter of a more traditional 'macho politician', she described how her powerful father had always accepted her as a daughter and encouraged her to follow him into politics and fight for transgender and LGBTQ+ people to be understood and treated as equal.

In 2017 she finally found herself giving her inaugural speech to the Philippine parliament. The topic was a bill that she had co-authored, called the Anti-Sexual Orientation or Gender Identity Discrimination Act, that had been stuck in political limbo for seventeen years. After a moving speech she received a standing ovation and the bill eventually passed the house unanimously.

Roman continues to battle for marriage reform despite acknowledging that the majority of Filipinos remain unaccepting of same-sex marriage. At the time of writing, she has a bill for civil unions before the courts.

If my father could hear me now, I would tell him this: 'Daddy, you and I need not beg my colleagues for respect. I am glad and proud that the members of the 17th Congress have not only welcomed me with open arms. They have dealt with me as a full-fledged colleague, as an equal'....

But I also speak before you on a matter of collective significance.... How can I turn a blind eye to the suffering that I myself have experienced at some point in my life?

Dear colleagues, you know who we are. We are your brothers, we are your sisters, your sons and your daughters, and nieces and nephews ... We are part of society.... We love our families. We love our country. We are proud Filipinos, who just happen to be LGBT.

The question now is: do we, as members of the LGBT community, share the same rights as all other citizens? Does the State grant us equal protection under our laws?

... Recognizing our rights and dignity will in no way diminish yours. We are not asking for special privileges or extra rights. We simply ask for equality. With inclusiveness and diversity, our nation has so much to gain ... The time ... is NOW.

SENATOR PENNY WONG

Australian Politician
b. 1968

As the world slowly shudders through to the inevitable logic of recognizing that marriage is an entitlement that should be available to all, one of the few benefits is that political leaders in the LGBTQ+ community have a moment to shine. Penny Wong is an openly gay member of the Australian Senate and has two children with her partner Sophie. She has often spoken bluntly, as is the tradition of Australian politics, on the topic of marriage and parenthood.

In this 2017 speech, the Australian government was trying to sidestep the issue of same-sex marriage by taking a postal plebiscite – a public survey via post to establish support for legislation – claiming it would 'unite the nation'. This did not turn out to be the case, despite the majority of respondents voting in support. As Wong emotionally predicts in her speech, the plebiscite created an environment in Australia that encouraged hatred and discrimination, which hurt not just LGBTQ+ people but also their families, their friends, and most of all their children. In her speech, Wong makes a reference to adopted children of LGBTQ+ parents being called a 'stolen generation' by Lyle Shelton of the Australian Christian Lobby, which was an electrifying dog-whistle to the community. It subtly reminded all white Australians of their own complicity in the horrors of the original stolen generation (a mass displacement of Indigenous Australian children), yet simultaneously expressed the disgust people felt towards the phrase being used as a corollary to LGBTQ+ adoption. By drawing attention to the awkward connotations of this phrase, Wong aptly demonstrates the divisiveness of the political discussion around this topic at that time in Australia.

You talk about unifying moments? It is not a unifying moment. It is exposing our children to that kind of hatred.

———

Senator Penny Wong

I Object ... To Being Told Our Children Are A 'Stolen Generation'

Canberra, Australia

9th August 2017

The reality is this is all a stunt and everybody knows that.... There are a lot of things you could do with $120 million: GP visits, more teachers. I am sure we can go through a whole range of things that $122 million can be spent on....

We are elected to do a job.... We are elected to come here and vote, to make decisions. This country didn't have a plebiscite or a postal ballot on the Racial Discrimination Act, the Sex Discrimination Act, native title legislation, scrapping of the 'White Australia Policy', whether women should get equal pay.... I don't think the government took to a people's vote whether corporations should get a big tax cut, but on this they want us to have our say.

Senator Cormann [said] this could be a unifying moment and that people could be respectful. I hope that people watching me in this debate would not think I am a shrinking violet. I know what a hard debate is like. But I tell you, have a read of some of the things which are said about us and our families and then come back here and tell us this is a unifying moment. The Australian Christian lobby described our children as the stolen generation. We love our children. And I object, as does every person who cares about children, and as do all those couples in this country, same-sex couples who have kids, to be told our children are a stolen generation. You talk about unifying moments? It is not a unifying moment. It is exposing our children to that kind of hatred.

I wouldn't mind so much if you were prepared to speak out on it. If the Prime Minister was prepared to stand up and say 'that is wrong'. Maybe he can stand up for some people who don't have a voice. Because we know the sort of debate that is already there. Let me say, for many children in same-sex couple families and for many young LGBTI kids, this ain't a respectful debate already.

CECILIA CHUNG

*Policy Maker, American Advocate for
Human Rights and LGBTQ+ Equality*
b. 1965

Women's March 2018

San Francisco, California, USA
22 January 2018

Cecilia Chung is a long-standing activist within the American LGBTQ+ community on the West Coast. Since 1998 she has been a prominent advocate for transgender health care and HIV/AIDS awareness. Chung has been notable as one of the first openly HIV-positive people to chair the San Francisco Human Rights Commission, and for her work on behalf of trans people as part of the Health Commission in the city. Chung's personal life story echoes that of many queer people of the last century. Coming out as transgender in the early 1990s, she lost her job and was estranged from her family before ending up homeless and drug-addicted on the streets of San Francisco, relying on risk-heavy sex work for an income. She experienced violence and harassment until reconciling with her family in the late 1990s, when she began the advocacy work that would make her an admired and visible Asian-American role model within the LGBTQ+ community.

In her speech given at the San Francisco Women's March in January 2018, Chung referred to the deaths of two trans women already that year; the number would rise to twenty-six in the US, and the American Medical Association would describe the situation as 'an epidemic'. In the speech, Chung highlighted that the struggle against domestic violence existed for all women.

When I first came to this country I knew I had to come to San Francisco because I knew this was the place I could call home. It was the most tolerant place about forty years ago.... Here in the United States we have a lot of advancement and I really appreciate all the wonderful things that all of you have provided for my beloved community. People living with HIV and transgender people – whether they're men or women – they get to be seen as your equals, they get to be treated vas equals.

... So why can't our ruling party do the same good deeds? To treat us all as equal? Why do the ruling parties continue to persecute women because they want to control how we make decisions for our bodies? How we make decisions for our life? How we make decisions for our family? That needs to stop. Our body is not up for negotiation. How we lead our lives is our business and not some legislators' or the White House's.

... It's not their decisions to make. We are not here to be objectified and we refuse to be objectified anymore. Just this year ... we have seen two trans women both get murdered. They were both murdered by their intimate partners.... When we talk about #metoo, let's talk about ending the violence that comes with it, otherwise we are doing a half-ass job. Let's make sure that our children have a great city and a world to live in.

HANNE GABY ODIELE

Belgian Model and Intersex Campaigner
b. 1988

Hanne Gaby Odiele came out publicly as intersex in January 2017 in order to be more transparent in campaigning for the need for intersex awareness. She used the media coverage both to educate and inspire, with rousing words that call for pride in being intersex, words that are echoed through this book in other speeches irrespective of the age. 'It is time for intersex people to come out of the shadows, claim our status, let go of shame, and speak out against the unnecessary and harmful surgeries many of us were subjected to as children.'

Odiele's status as intersex is not unique, however it remains stigmatized and misunderstood. As an endocrine condition rather than sexuality or gender orientation, intersex people have long been marginalized and under-supported within the LGBTQ+ community. Intersex people should be able to count on every member of the community as allies regardless, and in her 2018 *Teen Vogue* speech, Odiele outlined the many intersections within the LGBTQ+ community.

What is Intersex?

Teen Vogue Summit, New York City, USA

2nd June 2018

My name is Hanne Gaby, and last year I shared with the world I'm intersex. Intersex is the 'I' in LGBTQIA+. Are you guys familiar with what that entails?

... For the people that don't know, intersex is when you [are] born with physical sex characteristics that don't really fit in the definition of male and female. That can be through chromosomes, genitals, internal reproductive organs, etc. It's an umbrella term for many different traits. In fact, about 1.7 per cent of people are born intersex – [a] similar amount to people born with red hair.

... Like others in LGBTQ+ community, we face oppression because our bodies don't fit into society's binary structure. We don't just face discrimination but physical attacks on our healthy bodies.

... The medical community has been trying to erase our intersex bodies from society so we could fit into the binary standard. Infants and babies are subjected to unconsented, medically unnecessary and harmful surgeries that cause lasting physical and emotional damage.

... The UN and many other human rights organizations have labelled these surgeries as human rights violations, and even a form of torture.

... Still these surgeries are continually practised all over the world. For instance ... right here at Mount Sinai hospital, just down the road from here.

... To help stop these human rights abuses against intersex children, I partnered with interACT advocates, an organization fighting against intersex genital mutilation, and raising awareness about intersex rights.

... Intersex people also suffer oppression in other ways. Those who want legal recognition often cannot fit in with government documents that don't represent our expansive identities, beyond the binary.

... [We are] also often sensationalised in the news. People who compete in sports, especially intersex women of colour get rejected or asked to hormonally alter their bodies in order to comply to an imaginary concept of what it means to be a 'real' woman.

... I'm here to ask you to show up for intersex rights.

... Please include us in your conversation!

...Like others in LGBTQ+ community, we face oppression because our bodies don't fit into society's binary structure.

———————————

Hanne Gaby Odiele

OLLY ALEXANDER

British Musician, Actor and LGBTQ+ Activist
b. 1990

Olly Alexander is a British musician and actor who has talked openly and passionately about mental health and being gay. Alexander has leveraged his public presence to emerge as something our age understands with increasing clarity: the notion of an activist who is an artist, rather than a singer who is gay. The activist in him talks of depression and anxiety, eating disorders, hallucinations, self-harm and suicide. The artist speaks of love and longing.

The performance of the gay speech has changed dramatically in the last two decades. Gone is the shame or shared outrage, instead speakers are heroes and 'ambassadors' for the LGBTQ+ community. They stand without fear on stages, like, say, Glastonbury Festival's. Olly Alexander gave an empowered speech during his set, filling tens of thousands of under-slept eyes with unexpected tears as he pushed upon them the joy he felt in being allowed to be himself, a gay man.

The speech is particularly fascinating for the way it fixes a point of difference between those who came before him and those who will come after – with full awareness that the stage is not a rally, it is not a rousing pulpit address. Yet he uses it that way, reminding us that it's still not over – there is more work to be done for so many. We can, all of us, change history.

Queer is Beautiful

Pyramid Stage, Glastonbury, Somerset, UK
30th June 2019

You might have already noticed some of the subtle messaging on stage, [behind Alexander 'Queer is Beautiful' appears in huge letters]

But I'm gay and I talk about being gay kind of a lot. I'm sure some people wish I would shut up about it sometimes, but I have my reasons and some of them are personal, because I spent a lot of time wishing I wasn't gay, being ashamed of that, so now it's like I'm making up for lost time, you know?

The only reason I'm able to be up here talking about my gay self is because of all the people who came before me that fought for the rights of lesbian, gay, bisexual and transgender people. Sometimes we are referred to as the acronym LGBT, sometimes LGBTQ+, I personally like to use the word queer … but lots of people don't like that word, and that's because the word has a complicated and painful history and whether we like it or not, history really matters.

The reality is that the lives of LGBT people are as varied and complex as anyone else's, but they are under a very real threat. The fight for equality began before the Stonewall riots, it continues today and it will go on until tomorrow, into the future. But the future is not fixed. And our histories cannot predict what tomorrow might bring or what we might do with it.

I believe that everybody here has the chance to change history. We change history every day, and it's up to each and every one of us if we want to change the world. I believe there is no true LGBT equality until the fight against racism is over, against sexism is over, against ableism, bigotry, climate change… if we want to get anywhere without leaving anybody behind, we're going to have to help each other out.

I believe there is
no true LGBT equality
until the fight against
racism is over, against
sexism is over, against
ableism, bigotry,
climate change...

Olly Alexander

MUNROE BERGDORF

British Transgender Activist and Model
b. 1987

In the late 1990s the UK moved from a Conservative to a Labour government and enacted an agenda of socially progressive legislation. For the queer community this meant seeing the repeal of Section 28, a law prohibiting the teaching of LGBTQ+ in schools, the lowering of the age of consent for gay men and a gender recognition act [GRA] in 2004 that created a legal process for transgender people. For a few years, Cool Britannia was also Queer Britannia.

Some twenty years later, the generation of gender non-conforming folk that benefitted from this have emerged in response to a wave of transphobic and homophobic hostility. Model Munroe Bergdorf, author Shon Faye, activist/manicurist Charlie Craggs, columnist Paris Lees, food writer Jack Monroe, musician/writer CN Lester, and political activist Lily Madigan are just a few of the visible and vocal role models for a newly liberated generation of trans kids and their parents in the UK. These extraordinary young people are heirs to Marsha P. Johnson and Sylvia Rivera (see pages 28–31), a genesis of sass, queer theory, intersectional ideals, general fabulousness and lived trans experience – voices that have literally grown up online in the face of 'gender critical' rhetoric and the damaging and divisive maelstrom of 'trans-exclusionary radical feminism'.

The speech given by Bergdorf at the 2019 Women's March in London was not about trans exclusion; it was exactly the opposite. It was a speech of blatant solidarity in the face of open hostility from its own community.

No Woman Left Behind

Women's March, London, UK

19th January 2019

It is crucial that in this time of reduced social empathy, austerity, fake news and institutionalised bigotry, that NO woman is left behind. The myth that there are only so many seats at the table, is exactly that, a myth.

In the words of the late, great Shirley Chisholm, 'If they don't give you a seat at the table, bring a folding chair.' Well ... I would further that statement, by suggesting we bring our own table, a table with enough room for everyone. A table with no hate, a table with no prejudice, a table where everybody eats....

Because right now a great deal of women are going without and that has to stop.

Austerity hurts women.

It is the common denominator in a seemingly endless list of oppressive systems, from violence against women and girls, to racism, to Brexit.

Austerity must end and that starts with US!!!!!! WE CANNOT GET IN OUR OWN WAY.

All women must be equal. Our differences must be acknowledged and celebrated. All women must have a voice.

The rampant transphobia within the British press must stop.

The demonisation of transgender children under the guise of gender critical feminism, must STOP.

The dehumanisation of migrant women and children must END.

The targeting of sex workers through the implementation of brothel laws, must END.

All women deserve to feel safe, and right now SO MANY of us are scared, angry, frustrated and vulnerable. Today we march for every single woman who can't.

This is our opportunity to use our collective rage to make change happen for others, not just ourselves, but our sisters across the country and across the world.

We are strong and by God are we angry, but there are so many of us.

I want to leave you with this. I want you to join hands with the woman standing next to you. I want you to join hands and after three, I want to turn us all to promise that you will be there for not only the women you know and women like yourself, but also complete strangers who you have never met.

Repeat after me: 'I stand by you my sister.' 1, 2, 3...

...'I stand by you my sister'.

Munroe Bergdorf

MORE VOICES TO INSPIRE

It seems unnecessary to say that this anthology is just one perspective on LGBTQ+ history. Besides, history is a very fuzzy and imprecise thing to look at. We have included a tiny number of the many amazing folk who have stood up for themselves and for community across time. And we may have misquoted some of them. Standing up and speaking your truth is hard. If you liked their stories, here are a few more inspirational queers you may enjoy reading about.

OSCAR WILDE

My friends assumed that an Oscar Wilde speech would be included in this book, but in fact Wilde never acknowledged being homosexual nor spoke about 'gay rights'. It was illegal at the time, but also the words themselves had not been created to describe the idea of a gay identity, let alone the right to exist. In 1895, Wilde was put on trial for homosexuality and questioned extensively about 'the love that dare not speak its name'. He was eventually convicted of gross indecency, sentenced and imprisoned.

MAGNUS HIRSCHFELD

Magnus Hirschfeld should be the most famous white man in the history of LGBTQ+ activism. Prompted by the attempted suicide rate among his homosexual patients, the sexologist spent most of his career researching gay subcultures around the world and advocating for gay and transgender rights in pre-Nazi Germany. In 1933, an infamous Nazi book-burning incident targeted his research centre, the Institute for Sexual Research, destroying decades of LGBTQ+ history and research. With Hirschfeld we see the emergence of arguments that are still debated today on queer and gender 'debates'. Is it the individual who is defective or the societal response that creates stigma and shame?

LILI ELBE

Lili Elbe was a Danish painter and transgender woman who was a pioneer of trans identities in pre-war Europe. She successfully had her name and sex legally changed and was sometimes introduced in public as the sister of her artist wife Gerda. She also famously modelled for Gerda's paintings. In 1930, Elbe went to Germany for a series of sex reassignment surgeries; an infection resulting from the fourth operation in 1931 led to her death. Her life was later romanticized in the film *The Danish Girl* (2015).

JAMES BALDWIN

James Baldwin is possibly the most famous black gay American man to never give a speech about being gay, or homosexuality. Baldwin possessed extraordinary oratorical skills, a fluid wit and precision with language that he used to skewer opponents during the Civil Rights debates of the 1950s and 60s. In 1956 his novel, *Giovanni's Room*, brought both success and notoriety for its vivid homosexual themes.

BARBARA GITTINGS AND KAY LAHUSEN

Barbara Gittings and Kay Lahusen are essential characters in the era of American LGBTQ+ activism before the 1969 Stonewall riots. In 1958, Gittings founded the New York City chapter of the Daughters of Bilitis, a 'secret social club for lesbians'. After running the branch, she took over as editor of *The Ladder*. Lahusen, the first openly lesbian photojournalist who took many iconic images of the era, became her partner. Their post-Stonewall activism led to the American Psychiatric Association decision to remove homosexuality from the Diagnostic and Statistical Manual of Mental Disorder's list of mental illnesses. They also created the 'Hug a Homosexual' kissing booth at the American Library Association annual conference in 1971 which generated a media storm that highlighted gay rights issues.

LARRY KRAMER

An influential American gay writer, playwright and activist, Larry Kramer's plays were uncompromising and seen as excessive by both the art world and also the mainstream gay movement which objected to his sexualized representations of gay lifestyles. In 1987, in frustration at the apathy and bureaucracy surrounding the AIDS crisis, he founded ACT UP (AIDS Coalition to Unleash Power), the radical direct-action protest movement that arguably changed the world's perception of AIDS and influenced US policy.

MISS MAJOR GRIFFIN-GRACY

Miss Major Griffin-Gracy is a dynamic and vivacious activist and community leader, and a third sister to Sylvia Rivera and Marsha P. Johnson. By most accounts, Miss Major had a very tough upbringing, serving jail time in Chicago and later New York City. She was arrested during the Stonewall riots and beaten by the police. Later in life Miss Major became an AIDS activist in San Diego and San Francisco, and ran a

transgender support group for women in the justice system.

MARSHA P. JOHNSON

Marsha P. Johnson was a highly recognizable, charismatic gay rights activist and trans woman of colour in New York. Despite claiming not to have been present at the very start of the Stonewall riots, she has become an icon of LGBTQ+ rights post-Stonewall. A well-known figure on the streets, Johnson founded STAR with Sylvia Rivera (see pages 28–31), which supports young trans people, and was an AIDS activist in the 1980s. She modelled for Andy Warhol and was apparently known as the 'Mayor of Christopher Street' to her community.

BARBARA SMITH

Barbara Smith was a critical nexus in the black lesbian feminist movement of the 1970s and 80s. A writer and teacher, after becoming involved in the civil rights movement she remained focused on black lesbian feminist activism. In the 1980s she founded Kitchen Table: Women of Color Press, with lesbian writers of colour such as Audre Lorde (see pages 34–37) and Cherríe Moraga, in a successful attempt to overcome the absence of opportunity in publishing for women of colour.

PEDRO ALMODÓVAR

Pedro Almodóvar is an Oscar-winning Spanish director and screenwriter who directed many of the most iconic Spanish films over the past 40 years. Almodóvar's mainstream successes often explore LGBTQ+ themes without being explicitly about homosexuality, while his more niche films are very explicitly sexual. Many feature relationships between gay men and strong, often maternal, female leads, along with melodrama, bold colours, and unmistakeable camp. His work changed how Spanish cinema, Spain and LGBTQ+ representation are seen post-Franco.

STEPHEN FRY

Stephen Fry is an acclaimed British actor, author, comedian and polymath. As a visible, gay man he strongly influenced British perception having made documentaries on LGBTQ+ topics including *HIV and Me* (2007) and *Stephen Fry: Out There* (2013). In 2019, Fry spoke poignantly about his life as a gay man while receiving an honour for his activism. In addition, Fry is deeply respected for the frank way he addresses his bipolar disorder and his work around mental health issues.

KEITH HARING

Keith Haring was an internationally famous artist based in New York whose style grew out of his commitment to truly public art. Throughout the 1980s, Haring made work in subways and empty spaces that captured the pop art sensibility of the time. In 1990, he died at age 31 from AIDS-related complications after several years of LGBTQ+ activism, including founding the Keith Haring Foundation – a charity focused on educating young people about the risks of HIV/AIDS. He continues to be honoured for his work to this day.

JANE LYNCH

Jane Lynch is an American actress and comedian who had a long career in improv and indie comedies before having a late-career moment in the series *Glee*. Lynch has said that she never had a coming out moment simply because no one asked her, and she has promoted a more nuanced and thoughtful perspective on the values of tokenistic representation and labelling of queer people and other minorities in Hollywood.

WANDA SYKES

Wanda Sykes is an American comedian who came out by announcing that her wife was in the crowd at a 2008 rally for federal marriage equality. Previously she had been taciturn although privately open about her sexuality. As a queer black woman, she is an advocate of LGBTQ+ rights in her comedy work and was an outspoken and passionate campaigner for gay marriage.

LANA WACHOWSKI

Lana Wachowski was the first transgender person to direct a Hollywood blockbuster by continuing the *Matrix* series of films that she began in 1999 with her sister, Lilly Wachowski. Together they are known as 'The Wachowskis'. Both Lana and Lilly transitioned mid-career and became symbols of trans awareness. Lana has spoken sympathetically about interpretations of the earlier *Matrix* films as relating to the nature and process of being trans and transitioning in contemporary society.

ELLEN DEGENERES

Ellen DeGeneres is an American comedian, producer and talk show host. In 1997 she famously came out as a lesbian simultaneously: on her sitcom *Ellen*, and in real life to Oprah Winfrey. Within a year, *Ellen* was cancelled and she did not work again for three years. In a commencement speech at Tulane University, DeGeneres commented that after coming out, 'I was getting letters from kids [who] almost committed suicide, but didn't because of what I did'. She hosted *The Ellen DeGeneres Show* from 2003–2022, and in 2007 she became the first openly gay person to host the Academy Awards.

LAVERNE COX

Laverne Cox is an American actress who has vociferously advocated for LGBTQ+ rights throughout her career. As a transgender woman of colour, she was repeatedly compelled to discuss the existence of trans people. In a 2019 interview with *The Advocate*, she summed up how tiring that becomes: 'I'm done debating whether trans is real. I'm real. I'm sitting here and I have lived experiences as a woman, as a woman of trans experience, as a black woman, and so

JAMES BALDWIN

MARSHA P. JOHNSON

KEITH HARING

OSCAR WILDE

I'm done with that and I know a lot of trans folks are done with that'.

ROXANE GAY

Black queer woman and cultural icon, Professor Roxane Gay has gained a worldwide following with her sharp, witty observational studies nested in fairytales. An openly bisexual woman, her writing addresses race, xenophobia, sexual violence and fatphobia, and ranges from memoir to essays to fiction, even writing LGBTQ+ characters for *Marvel* in the 'World of Wakanda' series. A nuanced observer, Gay frequently returns to an interrogation of the expectations placed on women by modern society.

MAKI MURAKI

Maki Muraki is a Japanese activist and consultant who runs the LGBTQ+ non-profit Nijiiro Diversity (Rainbow Diversity). In 2016, Japanese magazine *Nikkei Woman* awarded her the prestigious Woman of the Year award and she was praised for her work in changing the conservative Japanese societal outlook that LGBTQ+ people experience. Her impact was described as 'a paradigm shift'. She is a visible lesbian voice in media and an advocate for more inclusive and progressive attitudes in Japanese corporate culture.

KANAKO OTSUJI

Kanako Otsuji was Japan's first lesbian politician. She was also one of its youngest elected officials in a country where politics is numerically dominated by men. First elected in 2003, Otsuji came out publicly in her autobiography in 2005 and has moved in and out of political positions in the years since, alongside her LGBTQ+ activism. She is currently the first and only openly gay member of Japan's House of Representatives.

HANNAH GADSBY

Hannah Gadsby is an Australian comedian and a queer icon following her critically successful Netflix comedy special *Nanette*. She spoke repeatedly on her 'unexpected' role as a visible masc-presenting lesbian, and as a disabled and neurodiverse person. She is a contemporary hero of the battle against conservative attitudes towards LGBTQ+ issues. She has said: 'I deal with the responsibility of being out and proud and even loud as much as I possibly can, because there are people who need to see me', which is what this book is all about.

RUTH HUNT

Baroness Hunt of Bethnal Green, London was the CEO of the UK LGBTQ+ charity Stonewall for five important years from 2014–19. Stonewall is the largest LGBTQ+ equality body in Europe and is influential in policy making decisions. Hunt's stewardship of the organization saw a significant shift in orientation towards more marginalized aspects of the LGBTQ+ society, advocating for the rights of trans and non-binary people against a wave of media-driven transphobia in the UK.

JANET MOCK

Janet Mock is an American author, producer and transgender rights activist. Significantly, she is one of the first visible women of colour to transition during high school and become a prominent role model during the wave of trans awareness that occurred between 2012 and 2016. More than any other, Mock and her generation initiated the ongoing shift in gender roles and our understanding of them. Her autobiography, *Redefining Realness*, was published in 2014, she wrote and directed on *Pose* (2018) and in 2019 became the first openly transgender woman of colour to sign a deal with Netflix.

DERAY MCKESSON

DeRay Mckesson is an American civil rights activist and part of the Black Lives Matter movement. As with Bayard Rustin (see pages 46–49), Mckesson has acknowledged black gay erasure and in 2015 addressed it head on in a GLAAD speech, calling the phenomenon 'the quiet'. He opened that speech stating, 'I stand here as a proud Black gay man', yet his continued LGBTQ+ activism is barely referenced in a 2019 edit of his Wikipedia entry.

JANELLE MONÁE

Janelle Monáe is many things to many people: an American pop star, an actress, a style icon, a sci-fi nerd and a champion for LGBTQ+ civil rights. Her music and identity developed under the mentorship of Prince, and in 2011 she made it clear who her community was: 'What I want is for people who feel oppressed or feel like the "other" to connect with the music and to feel like "She represents who I am"'.

FRANK OCEAN

Frank Ocean is an American rapper and music producer. He is mentioned as a visible black gay man in an era when queer representation remains bound up in the toxic and narrow definition of American black masculinity that emerged from centuries of global slavery. Ocean is one of only a few famous black US men who are open about their sexual history. There were very few coming out 'speeches' or even speeches about being gay from black men prior to Ocean's Open Letter that he posted on Tumblr and in which he came out.

EVAN RACHEL WOOD

Evan Rachel Wood is an award-winning American actress who has spoken up since 2011 about her bisexuality and is an advocate for charities focused on sexual and domestic abuse. Bisexuality is often overlooked by the broader LGBTQ+ community, and there are few visible icons. Woods was an early voice and has continued to discuss her experiences, including in a powerful 2017 Human Rights Campaign speech.

JONATHAN VAN NESS

The only openly gay hairdresser to be mentioned in this book, Jonathan Van Ness's role as the expert in personal grooming on the TV show *Queer Eye* has led to a huge global profile. In 2019, Van Ness came out as non-binary and also as HIV positive, which catapulted him to the front-line of visibility for queer representation. He is an activist in political, health and LGBTQ+ issues.

PARIS LEES

An English journalist who became *Vogue*'s first transgender columnist, Paris Lees was also the first openly transgender guest on the BBC's flagship political programme *Question Time* in 2013. Lees is an important and moderating voice in the group of younger trans and non-binary folk pushing back on British transphobia. She described the trans community in 2018 as being under 'constant attack in Britain over the past few years'. She is still active in lobbying for trans rights and sex-worker rights.

CHARLIE CRAGGS

Charlie Craggs is a British trans activist, writer and broadcaster. She started her own grassroots project Nail Transphobia in 2015, travelling around the UK painting nails and talking to people about transgender issues. In her first book, *To My Trans Sisters*, she compiled an anthology of letters from transgender people directed to the next generation of trans youth. In 2018, Craggs was active in lobbying Unicode for the transgender pride flag emoji, which was approved in 2020.

CREDITS

Karl Heinrich Ulrichs
PHOTO: Courtesy of The History Collection / Alamy

Robert G. Ingersoll
PHOTO: Courtesy of Artokoloro Quint Lox Limited / Alamy

Anna Rüling
Courtesy of Michwael Lombardi-Nash

Sally Miller Gearhart
© Sally Miller Gearhart
PHOTO: - Papers, Coll 305, Special Collections and University Archives, University of Oregon Libraries. Eugene, Oregon 97403-1299.

Sylvia Rivera
Reprinted by permission of the Stonewall Veteran's Association. Speech transcribed by Miria V. Eisenherz
PHOTO: © Valerie Shaff

Franklin Kameny
From The Advocates, Should Marriage Between Homosexuals Be Permitted?, © 1974 WGBH Educational Foundation; openvault.wgbh.org/catalog/V_57993D38129A433AAD10C7B04D019EF6
PHOTO: © Greg Villet / Getty

Audre Lorde
Excerpt from From 'Sister Outsider' © 1984, 2007 Audre Lorde
PHOTO: © Jack Mitchell / Getty

Harvey Milk
Reprinted by permission of The Harvey Milk Archives - Scott Smith Collection, San Francisco Public Library
PHOTO: © Daniel Nicoletta / Prod.DB / Alamy

Harry Hay
Reprinted by permission of the Estate of Harry Hay
PHOTO: © Daniel Nicoletta

Bayard Rustin
© Estate of Bayard Rustin
PHOTO: © Alan Baum / New York Times Co. / Getty

Sue Hyde
© Sue Hyde
PHOTO: © Marilyn Humphries

Vito Russo
Reprinted by permission of the Russo Family.
PHOTO: Craig Golding / Fairfax Media Archives / Getty

Mary Fisher
© Abataka Foundation Inc.
PHOTO: © Per-Anders Pettersson / Getty

Sir Ian McKellen
Reprinted by permission of Ian McKellen
PHOTO: (c) Trinity Mirror / Mirrorpix / Alamy

Essex Hemphill
Reprinted by permission of The Frances Goldin Literary Agency
PHOTO: Collection of the Smithsonian National Museum of African American History and Culture, Gift of Ron Simmons, © Ron Simmons

Simon Nkoli
Transcript courtesy of the Simon Nkoli Collection (AM2623: F1) at GALA Queer Archives
PHOTO: © Simon Nkoli Collection (AM2623: H4.1) at GALA Queer Archives

Urvashi Vaid
© 1993 Urvashi Vaid
PHOTO: Getty

Eric Rofes
© Crispin Hollings
PHOTO: Courtesy of Crispin Hollings

Elizabeth Toledo
© Elizabeth Toledo
PHOTO: Courtesy of Elizabeth Toledo

Tammy Baldwin
Reprinted by permission of the office of Congresswoman Tammy Baldwin
PHOTO: © Bill Clark / CQ Roll Call / Getty

Justice Michael Kirby
© Justice Michael Kirby
PHOTO: © Mark Tedeschi

Evan Wolfson
© Evan Wolfson, founder of Freedom to Marry
PHOTO: Courtesy of Evan Wolfson

Paul Martin
Reprinted by permission of the House of Commons
PHOTO: © Karl Stolleis / Getty

Ian Hunter
Reprinted by permission of the office of the
Hon. Ian Hunter
PHOTO: © Sergio Torres / AP / Shutterstock

Dan Savage and Terry Miller
Reprinted by permission of Dan Savage & Terry
Miller
PHOTO: © Jeff Vespa / WireImage / Getty

Rabbi Sharon Kleinbaum
© Rabbi Sharon Kleinbaum
PHOTO: © Erik McGregor / Pacific Press /
   LightRocket / Getty

Hillary Rodham Clinton
Reprinted via the U.S. Department of State
PHOTO: © Richard Ellis / Alamy

Arsham Parsi
© Arsham Parsi
PHOTO: © Megan Mack / Getty

Anna Grodzka
© Anna Grodzka
PHOTO: © WG PHOTO / Alamy

George Takei
© George Takei
PHOTO: © Jerritt Clark / WireImage / Getty

Debi Jackson
© Debi Jackson
PHOTO: © Dimitrios Kambouris / Getty for
   The Trevor Project

Jóhanna Sigurðardóttir
© Jóhanna Sigurðardóttir
PHOTO: © Halldor Kolbeins / AFP / Getty

Lee Mokobe
© 2018 Lee Mokobe. Some rights reserved.
PHOTO: Courtesy of Lee Mokobe

Alison Bechdel
© 2015 Alison Bechdel
PHOTO: © Everett Collection Inc / Alamy

Barack Obama
obamawhitehouse.archives.gov/the-press-
office/2015/06/26/remarks-president-supreme-
court-decision-marriage-equality
Reprinted under Creative Commons Attibution 3.0
PHOTO: © Winn McNamee / Getty

Sir Elton John
Reprinted by permission of Rocket Entertainment
PHOTO: © Trinity Mirror / Mirrorpix / Alamy

Ban Ki-moon
As published on www.un.org
PHOTO: © Giles Clark / Getty

Loretta E. Lynch
Transcript courtesy of the Department of Justice
PHOTO: © Andrew Harrer / Bloomberg / Getty

Geraldine Roman
© Geraldine Roman
PHOTO: © Francis R Malasig / EPA / Shutterstock

Senator Penny Wong
Reprinted by permission of the office of Senator
Penny Wong
PHOTO: © Mark Graham / Bloomberg / Getty

Cecilia Chung
© Cecilia C. Chung PHOTO: © Monica Schipper /
Getty

Hanne Gaby Odiele
© Hanne Gaby Odiele
PHOTO: © Lisa Maree Williams / Getty

Olly Alexander
Reprinted by permission of Olly Alexander
PHOTO: © Anthony Harvey / Shutterstock

Munroe Bergdorf
© Munroe Bergdorf
PHOTO: © SOPA Images Limited / Alamy

ACKNOWLEDGEMENTS

Thank you to David Breuer at Quarto for inviting me in and Kerry Enzor at White Lion Publishing for believing in the project. Zara Anvari, Phillipa Wilkinson, and Charlotte Frost – my wonderful editors who hand-held patiently and encouragingly, who found all the good speeches, and who coped with assorted episodes of me disappearing and reappearing over a rather complicated 18 months in my life.

Kerry Glencorse at Susanna Lea Associates who returned perfectly on time, as all good agents do, and without whose gentle prodding, patience, and perspicacity I would be lost.

Sam Turner and Katrina Dodd who I love dearly and who have heard far more about this project than they would probably like.

Fiona Wright for her insights on writing acknowledgements & Bea Star for bringing me into her cosmos with love and joy.

Andy Berndt and Alison Lord at Google who make the things I do in life possible, inside and outside work hours.

Nina, Gela and Tris for continuing to support me throughout and building a perfect world for my darling boys.

My parents, and my siblings back in the UK who would have helped if I'd let them, so I didn't.

I have too many friends to thank, and too messy a memory to remember everyone's contributions. But thank you.

Thanks to Laura Jordan-Bambach, Anna Turley, Chloe Hope, Mel Exon, Cecelia Herbert, Maria Popova, Lily Cole, Domino Pateman, Chloe Gottlieb, Edwina Throsby, Debbie Millman & Roxane Gay, Tina Roth Eisenberg, Amie Snow, Juliette La Montagne, Ashley Ford, Nancy Bennet, Cheyney Robinson, Naresh Ramchandani and Clare Corbould.

Thanks to my LGBTQ+ family, including Blair Imani, Rosie Lourde, Kaki King, Vesna Trobec, Adam JK, Charlie Craggs, Ben Law, Kate Morross, Liz Jackson, Alice Richard, Lily Madigan, CN Lester, Grace Franki, David Harris, John Gerrard, Lizi Hamer, Tara McKenty, Katelyn Burns, Bronwyn and Coco, Sue and Annabel, Amanda Jette Knox, Asad Dhuna, Chris Kenna, Linda Riley and DIVA, GLAAD, Maeve Marsden and Queer Stories, Twenty10, Helen and Mermaids, Pinnacle Foundation, Stonewall, Second Shelf Books, literally everyone at Kooky, and the queer bubble that is Sydney's inner west for letting me feel that I am, finally, OK.

The publisher would like to thank Dr Francis White for their valuable insight and advice.